HELP! THE MAC ANSWER BOOK

by Dr. Steven Schwartz, PhD.

alpha books

A Division of Prentice Hall Computer Publishing
11711 North College, Carmel, Indiana 46032 USA

International Standard Book Number: 1-56761-033-1
Library of Congress Catalog Card Number: 92-74694

95 94 93 92   8 7 6 5 4 3 2 1

Interpretation of the printing code: the rightmost double-digit number is the year of the book's printing; the rightmost single-digit number is the number of the book's printing. For example, a printing code of 92-1 shows that the first printing of the book occurred in 1992.

Printed in the United States of America

Marie Butler-Knight
Publisher

Elizabeth Keaffaber
Managing Editor

Lisa A. Bucki
Product Development Manager

Stephen R. Poland
Acquisitions Manager

Lisa C. Hoffman
Production Editor

Audra Gable, Barry Childs-Helton
Copy Editors

Hilary J. Adams
Editorial Assistant

Dan Armstrong
Cover Designer

Amy Peppler-Adams
Designer

Steve Vanderbosch
Illustrator

Jeanne Clark, Joy Dean Lee
Indexers

Katy Bodenmiller, Laurie Casey,
Tim Cox, Mark Enochs, Tim Groeling,
Phil Kitchel, Tom Loveman,
Carrie Roth, Kelli Widdifield
Production Team

Special thanks to Neil Day of
Apple Computers for ensuring the
technical accuracy of this book.

To Macintosh novices everywhere—and the computing hell that we all must occasionally endure.

Steve Schwartz spends the major part of each day getting a CRT tan. He is of the firm belief that one can never have too many computers, dogs, birds, or doughnuts.

Steve Vanderbosch, professional artist and travel afficionado, likes to snorkel in the Caribbean with his wife Julie.

Contents

Help! Table

Error Messages and Icons

This table lists the common error messages and icons Mac users may encounter, and gives the page number where you can find solutions.

Introduction

The Mac is not an appliance.

Whether you just bought your Mac or have had it for several years, you've already discovered that it is *not* an appliance. With an appliance, the range of potential problems is fairly limited. A toaster, for example, either toasts bread properly, requires a slight adjustment of an external control to make the toast lighter or darker, or it doesn't toast at all.

The Mac (or *any* computer, for that matter) is considerably more complex, as are the types of problems that can occur. Instead of knobs and dials, many of the controls you must use are in software. And any particular problem may be related to your equipment (the Mac, NuBus cards, external devices, and cables), to the software (the programs, extensions, and system software you use), or to a combination of the two. To get a Mac to work smoothly requires much more effort and brain power than simply knowing where the on/off switch is located.

When things go wrong (and they will), it's often difficult to know what you should do to resolve the problem: call your dealer, talk to a software publisher's technical support group, or try to diagnose and correct it yourself. *Help! The Mac Answer Book* uses a simple *problem/solution* approach to describe dozens of the most common Mac problems, offering concrete suggestions on how to fix them and, in some cases, how to *avoid* them. It also lets you know when it's time to call in the experts.

The purpose of *Help! The Mac Answer Book* is to:

- Teach you some elementary troubleshooting techniques that will help you determine the nature and cause of each problem.

- Show you how to correct many common problems by yourself.

- Help you determine which problems you can fix and which ones are best handled by your dealer.

No one expects you to start doing your own computer hardware repairs nor is that the purpose of this book. Many Mac problems, however, can be diagnosed and corrected by almost anyone. All you need is the willingness to try and a copy of this book as your guide.

Why should you do it yourself? Because if you don't, you'll waste time cursing at your Mac and waiting for your dealer to call-back. And time spent in this manner is time better spent in productive computing.

Like other Alpha books, *Help! The Mac Answer Book* was written with the novice user in mind. While it is not necessary to be a Mac hardware or software expert to benefit from this book, you will need to understand the basics of operating a Mac, such as using the mouse, running programs, and opening and saving files. If you need to brush up on the Mac essentials, you should skim through the owner's manual that came with your Mac, or pick up Alpha's *The First Book of the Mac,* Second Edition, by Carla and Jay Rose.

A discussion of networks and network-specific problems is beyond the scope of this book. Nevertheless, many of the troubleshooting techniques presented will also be useful for Macs on a network. (Software bugs and system crashes can affect any Mac, whether it's a stand-alone unit or is connected to a network.)

Acknowledgments

There are many people I'd like to thank for helping with the creation of this book:

Matt Wagner, my agent at Waterside Productions, and Stephen Poland, Acquisitions Manager of Alpha Books, for selecting me to write the book,

The hard-working, friendly, *cooperative* editors at Alpha Books: Lisa Bucki, Product Development Manager; Faithe Wempen, Development Editor; Lise (Lisa) Hoffman, Production Editor; as well as Audra Gable and Barry Childs-Helton, Copy Editors,

Neil Day, Apple Computer, who graciously volunteered to serve as Technical Editor, and

My wife, kids, and dogs for tolerating the mess in my office long enough for me to finish the book.

Trademarks

All terms mentioned in this book that are known to be trademarks or service marks are listed below. In addition, terms suspected of being trademarks or service marks have been appropriately capitalized. Alpha Books cannot attest to the accuracy of this information. Use of a term in this book should not be regarded as affecting the validity of any trademark or service mark.

911 Utilities is a trademark of Microcom Systems, Inc.

Adobe Illustrator and PostScript are registered trademarks and Adobe Type Manager is a trademark of Adobe Systems Incorporated.

After Dark and More After Dark are trademarks of Berkeley Systems.

Apple File Exchange, AppleShare, Apple SuperDrive, Disk Copy, Disk First Aid, Extension Manage, HD SC Setup, HyperCard, MacDraw Pro, Macintosh Plus, SE, Classic, Portable, and PowerBook, II series and Quadra, TrueType fonts are trademarks of Apple Computer, Inc.

AutoDoubler, DiskDoubler, and Fastback II are trademarks of Fifth Generation Systems, Inc.

CanOpener 2 is a trademark of Abbott Systems.

Central Point MacTools is a trademark of Central Point Software, Inc.

Disk Manager Mac is a trademark of Ontrack Computer Systems.

DiskExpress II is a trademark of ALSoft, Inc.

DiskFit Pro is a trademark of Dantz Development.

DiskMaker is a trademark of Golden Triangle.

DiskTop Find and Heap Fixer are trademarks of CE Software.

FileMaker Pro is a registered trademark of Claris Corporation.

Floppier is a trademark and Norton Utilities for the Mac is a registered trademark of Symantec Corporation.

GOfer is a trademark of Microlytics, Inc.

Help! is a trademark of Teknosys.

INITPicker, Redux, and Rival are trademarks of Microseeds, Inc.

MicroPhone II is a trademark of Software Ventures Corporation.

Microsoft Word is a registered trademark of Microsoft Corporation.

More Disk Space is a trademark of Alysis.

NOW Utilities and StartUp Manager are trademarks of NOW Software.

PageMaker and SuperPaint are registered trademarks of Aldus Corporation.

Retrospect is a trademark of Dantz Development.

SCSI Probe and SCSI Tools are trademarks of SyQuest Corporation.

Shortcut and StuffIt Deluxe are trademarks of Aladdin Systems.

Snooper is a trademark of Maxa Corporation.

SuperSpool and SuperLaserSpool are trademarks of SuperMac Software, a division of Scientific Micro Systems, Inc.

Basic Issues

This chapter is a grab bag of facts, suggestions, and tips that every Mac owner should know. Whether you just bought your Mac or have had it for several years, the information in this chapter will come in handy when selecting and installing new equipment, when troubleshooting software and hardware problems, and when using your Mac on a daily basis. Just as it is essential to learn how the mouse works in order to use a Mac, the information presented here is essential to avoiding and resolving Mac problems. Consider this the foundation for Macintosh Troubleshooting 101.

Topics covered in this chapter include:

- An introduction to Macintosh hardware.

- Safety precautions to follow when troubleshooting hardware problems.

- The correct way to start up and shut down your Mac.

- Hardware protection devices to prolong equipment life and protect your data.

- Proper equipment placement.

- Universal troubleshooting tips (things to try when you have no idea what's causing the problem).

A Hardware Walk-Through

Whether you set up the Mac yourself or were helped by a dealer or friend, you'll need to know—at least in general—what the different components are and what they do. Let's take a quick stroll through the components of your computer system. Figure 1.1 shows the parts of a typical system.

Figure 1.1

A typical Macintosh configuration. (Clip art courtesy of T/Maker Company.)

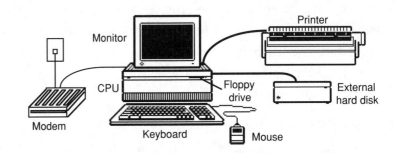

Because there are many different Macintosh models—as well as *peripherals* (devices that can be connected to the Mac)—your equipment array may be different. A basic system, however, always includes at least the following items:

- *CPU* or *Central Processing Unit*   The CPU is actually only a chip inside the Mac—its "brains." However, when people talk about the CPU, they are frequently discussing their particular Mac model and not the chip, because the terms *Mac* and *CPU* are often used interchangeably.

- *Monitor*   The screen on which you view data.

- *Disk drives* (one or more)   Devices for storing data and programs.

- *Keyboard*   You use it to type the characters that appear on-screen.

- *Mouse* or *trackball*   Pointing devices which enable you to perform on-screen operations, such as selecting files and moving the cursor.

Additional hardware you might own or eventually purchase can include a *printer* (a device for generating printed output from your programs—reports and business letters, for example), a *modem* (a device which enables you to communicate with other computers over standard phone lines), a *scanner* (converts real-world images, such as photographs, into graphic files that can be stored, viewed, and edited on the Mac), a *tape drive* (a backup device used to store copies of your critical data on cassette-style tapes), and additional disk drives (internal or external floppy drives, hard disk drives, removable cartridge drives, and CD-ROM drives).

What Everything Is and Does

If you open a popular computer magazine like *Macworld*, you'll see dozens of hardware ads offering add-ons for the Mac. If you aren't familiar with what the different devices do or how they might help you, the following information is for you. (Even if you consider yourself something of a hardware expert, skim through this section anyway. You may pick up a useful tidbit or two.)

Disk Drives

Disks store data and programs. When you store a file on disk by issuing a **Save** command, the file remains on disk, even when you turn off the power.

NOTE

New users often confuse a Mac's storage capacity with the amount of memory in the machine. Storage capacity refers to a Mac's total disk storage space, calculated by adding the capacity of all attached hard disks. The Mac's memory (also called RAM or Random Access Memory) is used to run programs and desk accessories and to manipulate data. Unlike disk storage, the contents of RAM disappear whenever you quit from a program or shut down the Mac. Memory is for temporary storage. Disks are for long-term storage.

The three basic types of disk drives are the *floppy drive, fixed hard disk,* and *removable hard disk. Floppy drives* are internal or external drives that use 3.5" removable disks. Because commercial software is usually distributed on floppy disks (also called *floppies*), almost every

Mac comes with a built-in floppy drive. The current Macintosh floppy drive is known as the *SuperDrive*. It can accommodate either of the two popular Mac-format floppies: 800K (double-sided, double density floppies) and 1.4M (double-sided, high-density floppies). With appropriate software, the SuperDrive can also read and write IBM disks. Other than its limited storage capacity, the floppy drive's biggest limitation is its speed. Floppy drives read and write data very slowly.

NOTE

Disk capacity and file sizes are often displayed and discussed in terms of K (kilobytes) or M (megabytes). Each K represents 1,024 bytes of data, and each byte corresponds roughly to one character. A megabyte is 1,000K—about one million bytes of data.

Although a Mac can operate entirely from floppy drives, few do. *System 7* (the current Macintosh system software version) is extremely difficult to run from a floppy disk, and the large storage requirements of many programs make floppy-based systems impractical.

With their impressive capacities, *fixed hard disks* are the preferred storage medium for most Macs. Like floppies, fixed hard disks can be internal or external units. Internal drives are mounted inside the Mac; external drives rest outside of the Mac and are connected in series by cables to the Mac's *SCSI* (Small Computer System Interface) port. (Figure 1.2 shows the icon for this port.) The storage capacity of fixed hard disks is rated in megabytes (M) and may vary from a low of 20M to as high as several *gigabytes* (1,000 megabytes equals 1 gigabyte).

Figure 1.2

This icon identifies your Mac's SCSI port.

Removable hard disk drives are now commonplace on Macs. Based on the SyQuest, Bernoulli, or Ricoh mechanism, removable hard disk drives use removable cartridges. Removable drives share many of the advantages of fixed hard disks, including relatively high storage capacity and data access speed that is only a little slower than that of fixed hard disks. Because they are removable, you can just buy another cartridge if you run out of disk space.

Two other storage technologies should also be mentioned. *Flopticals* (optical floppies) are a new breed of high-capacity floppy drive. Floptical disks can hold about 20M of data and, like floppies, are removable.

CD-ROM drives continue to grow in popularity. Using discs like those used to hold music for CD players, CD-ROMs can handle massive amounts of data (about 300M per disc), such as encyclopedias, huge product databases, and detailed graphics. The other storage devices discussed here can be written to by the user; that is, you can save files and programs on them. CD-ROMs, however, are purchased with the data already on them (as supplied by the software publisher) and are *read-only*. You cannot erase CD-ROM data or save new data to the discs. Compared to other technologies, CD-ROMs are *extremely* slow.

See Chapter 3 for more information about disk drives and disk-related troubleshooting.

Monitors

The monitor is the screen on which you view and manipulate all data. Some Macs (the Plus, SE, Classic, Portable, and PowerBook, for example) come with a built-in monitor. Others, such as the II series and Quadra, require that you purchase an external monitor that must be connected to the Mac's video port (if it has one), or to a video card or video adapter. Monitor/video card combinations can produce black-and-white, gray-scale, or color images—depending on the particular Mac, monitor, and video card you have. (See Chapter 6 for more information about monitors and video cards.)

Printers

If you need paper copies of memos, reports, worksheets, or any other information in your Mac, you'll need a printer. The three basic printer types are *dot-matrix, ink-jet,* and *laser. Dot-matrix printers* are impact printers. They form characters by causing patterns of pins in the printhead to strike an inked ribbon. When struck, the ink transfers from the ribbon to the paper. Dot-matrix printers, such as Apple's ImageWriter II, are slow, but can produce reasonably attractive output for a low price.

Ink-jet printers are next on the price and quality ladder. They work by shooting tiny jets of ink onto the paper. Although very slow, they can print images at the same resolution as most laser printers (300 dots per inch or *dpi*).

Laser printers create images on paper in much the same way as photocopiers do. Instead of using ink, special toner is fused to the paper to create text and graphics. With a minimum resolution of 300 dpi, lasers are frequently the product of choice for high-quality business correspondence, for example.

Laser printers usually support one of two imaging technologies: QuickDraw or PostScript. QuickDraw-based lasers create images directly from those that appear on-screen. (*QuickDraw* is the system software routine that is responsible for all on-screen images.) PostScript laser printers, on the other hand, can use any of the hundreds of high-quality PostScript fonts to print text, and can generate extremely detailed PostScript graphics. (See Chapter 5 for additional information about printers and printing problems.)

TIP

If you are only interested in impressive correspondence and reports, a QuickDraw laser can save you money. If you'll be using the printer for desktop publishing or graphics work, you'll be much happier with a PostScript laser. A few companies have also introduced TrueType laser printers that are based on Apple's new TrueType font technology. TrueType has one major advantage: a single TrueType font file can generate both on-screen and printed characters in an almost infinite number of sizes. PostScript outline font files are used to create printed characters only. Unless you also have a utility called ATM (Adobe Type Manager), screen fonts are generated from a second set of font files. PostScript, however, is widely used. If there was a vote for the technology that will win out, my money would be on PostScript.

Input Devices

The keyboard and mouse are the standard input devices for the Mac. The keyboard is used to type letters, numbers, and special symbols into the current document. The mouse is a pointing device that you use to select onscreen objects, highlight words, open files, launch programs, and so on. A *trackball* is a common alternative to the mouse. Although a trackball works the same as a mouse, it contains a ball that you roll within a stationary base. Mice must be physically moved around on your desk in order to translate their movements to the screen. (See Chapter 7 for further discussion of keyboards, mice, and trackballs.)

Modems and Fax-Modems

Modems allow you to exchange data with other computers or information services over standard phone lines. The word *modem* comes from the terms *MODulate* and *DEModulate*, which describes the communication process. The modem takes digital data from your computer, *modulates* it (changing it to analog data; that is, sounds), and transmits it over the phone line. The receiving modem then *demodulates* the sounds, converting them back to their original digital form so your computer can interpret the data. Modems can be used to exchange any type of file that exists in your Mac, including data files, graphics, and even programs. They also work over long distances, making them ideal for moving data across the country or to the other side of the world. "Modems—when overnight services are just too slow."

A *fax-modem* is a special type of modem that, in addition to transferring data from point to point, can also double as a Group III-compatible fax machine. (For additional information about modems and fax-modems, refer to Chapter 9.)

Now that you know what the basic hardware components of a Mac system are for, let's move on to some techniques for handling them, protecting them from damage, and troubleshooting problems that may arise.

A Hardware-Handling Primer

Whether you're troubleshooting a hardware problem, connecting a peripheral to your Mac, or installing more RAM, you don't want to hurt the equipment or yourself. Here are a few easy rules to follow when handling your Mac, its cables, and peripherals.

Rule #1: Cut the Power

Whether you are opening the case to make sure that accessory cards are properly seated or are just checking external cable connections, turn off all power to the Mac first. As an added precaution, you may want to unplug the power cords from their outlets—particularly when opening the Mac's case.

Also, try not to jostle your equipment when the power is on. Bumping a keyboard can dislodge a mouse or trackball cable that is plugged into it. Jarring a hard disk can result in data loss or a fatal—and expensive—head crash. Before rearranging your Mac and peripherals, always follow the Shut Down procedure (described below) and turn off the power.

Rule #2: When Opening the Case, Ground Yourself

The inside of a Mac II-series computer is no more dangerous than that of a PC. Rather than hurting yourself, the greater danger is to your Mac and to its components. This, however, is *not* true of the "sealed" Macs—the ones with built-in video, such as the Plus, SE, and Classic. Unless you're electronically adept, handling the innards of any Mac with built-in video is best left to qualified service technicians.

To avoid damaging your computer, it's important to discharge all static electricity before touching anything inside the Mac. For minor work inside a Mac II or any other Mac that has a pop-off cover, you can ground yourself by keeping one hand on the Mac's power supply. *Make sure that you obey Rule #1, though!* For more extensive work, you may want to invest in an inexpensive grounding strap. NuBus cards, cache cards, and RAM modules frequently come with a grounding strap and instructions for using it.

Rule #3: Know When It's Time to Call in the Experts

Depending on your facility with hardware and electronics, it's important to know when a hardware repair or upgrade is best handled by a trained professional.

Installing a NuBus card or attaching an external peripheral can be handled by almost anyone. If you have even a passing familiarity with a screwdriver and needle-nose pliers, you can safely remove unnecessary terminating resistors from a SCSI device (a hard disk or tape drive, for instance)—assuming that you can identify them. Installing almost anything inside a *sealed* Mac, on the other hand, is probably better left to the pros.

CAUTION

Keep in mind that messing with the innards of most Macs will void the warranty if it's still in effect.

Starting Up and Shutting Down

To avoid damage to your data files, programs, and system files, it's extremely important to shut down the Mac in the proper way. (It's a bad idea to just turn off the power.) Here's the *right* way to both start up and shut down your Mac.

Starting Up

1. Turn on all attached SCSI devices, and let them warm up.

   This refers to all devices attached to your Mac's SCSI port. Such devices often include hard disks, removable cartridge disks, tape drives, scanners, and CD-ROM units.

CAUTION

These are essential procedures—ones that you should treat as sacred. Unless a system crash or power failure prevents you from shutting down in the proper manner, for example, you should always follow these steps.

15

How can you tell when they're warmed up? In the case of a hard drive, you can usually tell just by listening. Most hard drives make a characteristic series of noises as they're going through their warm-up. Typically, the process takes between 20 seconds and a minute. If the device has a pair of drive lights (one red and one green), the drive is ready to go when the red light stops flashing and a steady green light appears.

Non-SCSI peripherals, such as printers and modems, usually don't need to be on at startup. Check their manuals to be sure.

TIP

Because external SCSI devices must be turned on separately from the Mac, you won't be able to hook everything to a single power strip—unless the strip has controls that allow you to turn on the peripherals separately from the Mac. You'll be better off shopping for a power control center, shown in Figure 1.3. Generally, a power control center is a large, flat box about two inches high. Its shape allows it to be placed under most Macs or used as a monitor stand. Power control centers usually sport between four and six switches that can be used to individually control the power to that number of devices. Better units also provide protection from power surges, and may include a phone jack you can use to protect a modem or fax-modem.

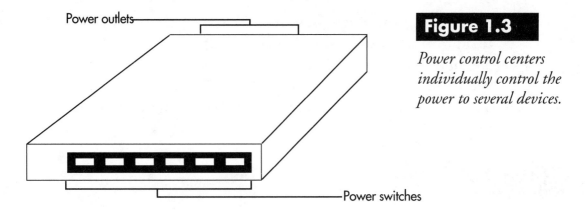

Power outlets

Figure 1.3

Power control centers individually control the power to several devices.

Power switches

2. Turn on your Macintosh.

   Depending on your equipment configuration, press the Mac's power switch or the power key on the keyboard (the one with the open triangle symbol on it).

Shutting Down

When shutting down the Mac, it's extremely important that you follow the steps in order. Failure to do so can result in damage to data and critical system files.

1. Quit all programs and choose **Shut Down** from the Finder's **Special** menu (see Figure 1.4).

Selecting the Shut Down command instructs the system software to quit from any programs that are still open, close all open files, and update the desktop information for each attached drive. This will automatically shut off some Macs. On others, it will present a dialog box with instructions for completing the shut down process.

Figure 1.4

The Special menu is used to shut down the Mac correctly.

2. If the Mac did not automatically shut off in the previous step, turn it off now.

3. Turn off any external drives and other equipment.

   Once the Mac is off, no more data needs to be written to your drive(s). It is then safe to turn them off.

Sometimes it may not be possible to use the Shut Down command. If your Mac has crashed or locked up, you may not be able to select Shut Down or even quit from the current application. There are other procedures you can try following a crash, described later in this chapter in "Universal Troubleshooting Tips."

Hardware Protection Devices

Other than praying that your hardware won't fail, there are inexpensive devices you can buy to protect your system and extend its working life. Which ones are essential and which you can do without depends mainly on conditions in your workplace.

Anti-Static Sprays, Mats, and Strips

If static electricity around your workspace is a problem (disks and electronic devices are all susceptible to static damage), there are several simple ways to combat it. First, there are sprays you can squirt on the floor surrounding your work area. Second, some chair mats can eliminate static. Third, there are electronic anti-static strips that can be mounted near your computer. As long as you touch the strip before handling any disks or touching your Mac, any static electricity in your body will be safely transferred to the strip where it can do no damage.

Surge Protectors and UPS

Following a power outage, a tremendous surge of electricity can rush into your wall outlets—and straight into any unprotected devices. One power surge like that can put the Mac or its peripherals out of commission. At a minimum, you should invest in some inexpensive surge protectors. If the current exceeds a safe amount (as it would during a surge), the surge protector self-destructs, keeping the electric surge from reaching your computer. Many power control centers (discussed in a tip earlier in this chapter) include surge protection.

There are many different devices that offer surge protection. The simplest (and usually cheapest) is a small cube-shaped device that plugs into the wall outlet. You can plug one or more devices into the surge protector, and it will protect them all. Better versions include an indicator light that shows that the surge protector is still working. Power strips often include built-in surge protection. When selecting a surge protector, look for one that offers "three-line protection" or protects against "common mode transients." These devices protect against surges between all three wires: hot, neutral, and ground.

For critical installations (network file servers and Macs used by sales or accounting departments, for instance), you might also consider buying a *UPS* (uninterruptable power supply). A UPS can provide one or two functions. A basic UPS is merely a large rechargeable battery that supplies several minutes of electricity during a power failure. When the electricity fails or drops below an acceptable level, the UPS kicks in, giving you time to save all open files, quit from programs, and shut down the equipment. Better UPS units also offer *line conditioning*. They regulate the line voltage that passes through them, making sure that your equipment always receives "clean" electricity—a constant voltage without peaks or valleys.

UPS systems are generally rated according to the number of watts they can handle. Before selecting one, be sure to add up the power requirements of all computer devices you intend to connect to the UPS.

TIP

Never include a laser printer in your UPS power calculations. First, a laser's power requirements are extremely high, which makes it impractical to run one through a UPS. Second, if there's an outage while you're printing, you can always pick up the print job where it left off. Thus, lasers should not be connected to a UPS; a surge protector will do just fine.

If betting on a constant stream of clean electricity is an "iffy" proposition in your neighborhood (it is in mine) or your workplace is subject to frequent brownouts or power failures, a UPS can be an excellent data- and hardware-saving investment.

Power Control Centers
See the description of these devices in the earlier section called "Starting Up."

Equipment Covers, Dust Removal Sprays, and Computer Vacuums

If you work in an extremely dusty environment or use your Mac infrequently, you may want to buy some inexpensive dust covers. (Otherwise, covers are a nuisance and you'll probably toss them in a corner after a couple of weeks.)

To get rid of dust *inside* your Mac, you may be tempted to buy a dust removal spray. Don't! Sprays generally use a liquid propellant to force air from the can. If you tilt the can too far, the propellant will mix with the jet of air. Comparatively speaking, your Mac would have been better off with the dust.

You can do a better, safer job of removing dust with a miniature or full-size data vacuum (they look like small canister vacuum cleaners). Some of the better units can also be used to collect toner spilled inside a laser printer. (Toner is extremely fine, so only special vacuums or ones fitted with special filters should be used to collect it.) The cost of the larger units (usually between $100 and $200) is normally warranted only for large computer installations.

Proper Equipment Placement

Aside from buying the hardware protection devices discussed above, one of the simplest ways to safeguard your hardware and data requires only that you arrange your equipment properly.

Hard disks, for example, should not be placed next to the Mac's power supply. The powerful magnets in the power supply can conceivably cause damage to the data on the hard disk. If your Mac owner's manual suggests a safe position for an external hard disk, heed it.

Monitor placement can also be important, particularly if you have two monitors. If you notice that one of the screens seems to be having an interference problem (images may waiver or appear distorted), try moving the monitors further apart. They may be interfering with each other.

Finally, use common sense when stacking peripherals on top of each other or placing equipment above or beneath the Mac. Many peripherals have slots in their sides or top to allow heat to dissipate. Do not block these vents—either by placing another peripheral on top of the vents or by shoving a peripheral up against a side vent. Excessive heat can substantially shorten equipment life.

Universal Troubleshooting Tips

Whether you suspect that a hardware or software problem is currently plaguing you, there are some simple troubleshooting techniques you can try before assuming that the problem is complex. Most of the techniques can be accomplished easily and quickly. Many of the troubleshooting tips in this book will refer you to the techniques discussed here.

Tip #1: Try It Again

Sometimes problems are one-time occurrences. Before deciding that you need some expensive repairs, that the system software should be reinstalled, or that you have discovered a software incompatibility, it's best to simply retry whatever you were doing when the problem occurred (printing a particular document, connecting by modem with an information service, or issuing a formatting command). If the problem disappears—and it often will—you can chalk it up to gremlins or a "glitch" and get back to work.

Tip #2: Cycle the Power (Hit the On/Off Switch)

If Tip #1 has no effect, quit from each open program, select **Shut Down** from the Finder's **Special** menu, and then turn off all your equipment. Leave the power off for at least 15 seconds before restarting your Mac.

Although printers and modems can often be reset with software commands, the most reliable way to reset a problematic piece of hardware is by turning it off and back on.

Tip #3: Turn Off Extensions (INITs)

Pieces of software called *extensions* (in System 7) or *INITs* (in System 6) can sometimes conflict with each other or cause programs and hardware to malfunction. To determine if an extension is the root of your problem, temporarily turn off all extensions, reboot your Mac, and then see if the problem recurs.

With System 7, you can turn off extensions by holding down the **Shift** key as you are booting. If successful, you should see a message informing you that all extensions are off. The next time you boot *without holding the Shift key*, the extensions will be back on.

If you are running System 6, there is no built-in shortcut for turning off INITs. To do this manually, start by opening your System Folder, then create a new folder called something like INIT Holder. (Press ⌘-**N** to create a new folder.)

Now select **By Kind** from the **View** menu. Any non-Apple file that is listed as a "Startup document" or "Control Panel document" should be dragged to the folder you just created. (Apple-provided Startup and Control Panel documents that you can ignore include: Easy Access, Responder, General, Keyboard, Map, Mouse, and Sound.) After dragging the files into the INIT Holder folder, you can reboot your Mac using the Special menu's **Restart** command.

Regardless of which version of system software you are using, if turning off the INITs/extensions and Control Panel documents makes the problem go away, you probably have a conflict involving at least one of these documents. See Chapter 3 for help in identifying the one causing the problem.

TIP

As extensions and Control Panel documents multiply in your System Folder, you'll be better off installing an extension manager utility, such as INITPicker (Microseeds Publishing) or StartUp Manager (part of the Now Utilities from Now Software). Extension managers allow you to selectively add or remove extensions without having to manually drag the files around.

Tip #4: Check the Cables

Modem, mouse, monitor, and hard disk problems can all be caused by loose or damaged connecting cables. Cable damage can range from the obvious (frayed wires or dangling connectors) to the invisible (a broken or frayed wire *inside* the cable's protective covering). If you suspect that you have a cable problem, shut down the Mac and all attached peripherals. Then disconnect and reconnect the appropriate cables. While checking cables, examine your power cords as well.

If the problem remains after you reboot, shut down again and replace any questionable cables with known good ones. (If possible, don't buy them—borrow them. There's no sense replacing cables unless you're sure that they're bad.)

Tip #5: Reinstall Suspect Software

Virtually any kind of file can become corrupted or damaged—especially following a system crash. If all your problems happen in one particular program or DA (desk accessory), reinstall a fresh copy of the program or DA from your original disks.

Before assuming that the program itself has been damaged, however, you might try throwing away any *preferences* file created by the program or DA. (Actually, *moving* the preferences file to a different folder will have the same effect.) Check in the following places for a preferences file: the program folder, the System Folder, and the Preferences folder within the System Folder. If a preferences file isn't found by the program when you run it, most programs will automatically create a new, clean one for you.

A more serious problem—and one that, unfortunately, seems to happen more often—is system software corruption. If the System file, Finder, or one of the other system software components becomes corrupted, you may experience problems at almost any time. See Chapter 2 for specific instructions for reinstalling a clean copy of the system software.

Tip #6: Swap It Out

This is precisely what many repair shops do when a hardware problem isn't easily diagnosed. If you suspect a bad cable, try a known good one in its place. If you aren't able to telecommunicate with your modem, try someone else's modem with your cable—or try his cable with your modem. After each test, you should be able to eliminate one piece of hardware or one cable from suspicion. (If the second modem works, for example, you know that your cable is okay.) With any sort of peripheral, cable, or card problem, swapping out components is often the fastest way to identify the one that isn't working correctly.

Tip #7: Use the Emergency Quit Command

When your Mac locks up (keeping you from saving current documents and gracefully quitting from programs), there is one last trick you can try before rebooting. Press ⌘-**Option-Esc**. This is an emergency quit command that will sometimes allow you to exit from the current program. Although current files will not be saved, you may be able to save open documents in *other* programs before shutting the Mac down.

Moving On

In this chapter, we covered the basic information necessary to understand the rest of the material in *The Mac Answer Book*. You learned about the different Macintosh hardware components, how to safely handle your hardware and protect it from damage, the proper way to start up and shut down the Mac, and how to do some elementary troubleshooting.

In Chapter 2, you'll find out about the Macintosh system software: what it is and does, the proper method for upgrading to a new version, and how to resolve problems involving the system software.

System- and System Software-Related Problems

This chapter covers the *big* problems. In addition to providing an introductory discussion about the Mac system software (and difficulties you may encounter), the chapter also includes troubleshooting tips for many of the really nasty system problems: startup problems, system crashes, memory problems, and computer viruses.

What Is "System Software?"

The system software drives the Mac and its peripherals. In conjunction with the software routines in your Mac's ROM (Read-Only Memory), the system software creates and organizes the desktop, enables the Mac to save and open files, draws text and graphics on your screen, and performs all the other niceties needed to keep your Mac running happily. The two main components of the system software are the *System* and *Finder*.

Under System 6 (a version of the system software), users could choose between two operating environments: Finder and *MultiFinder*. Under the Finder, the Mac allows only one program to run at a time. Under MultiFinder, users can run as many programs at one time as the Mac's memory will allow.

MultiFinder made it simple to move data between applications. You could easily copy and paste an image from a graphics file into a word processing document, for instance. Performing this task under the Finder would require that you:

1. Run the graphics program, open the document, and copy the graphic to the *Clipboard* (a storage area in RAM provided by the system software).

2. Quit from the graphics program.

3. Run the word processing program, open the document, and paste the graphic into the selected location.

System 7 no longer supports this dual Finder/MultiFinder mode of operation. MultiFinder is now a permanent part of the system software. You can still run one program at a time—quitting before starting a different one—but there is no requirement for doing so. As long as you have some free memory, you can run as many programs as you like.

In addition to the Finder and System files, the system software consists of a number of other components, such as the Apple-supplied CDEVs (for example, Sound, Memory, Color, and General Controls) and extensions (such as AppleShare, Network Extension, DAL, and printer drivers).

INITs (called extensions in System 7) are software routines that the Mac automatically runs at startup. Because they are available at all times, they are also referred to as background software. Common examples of INITs are device drivers, such as those used by CD-ROM drives and fax modems, and any other software that needs to be constantly available, such as macro utilities. CDEVs (control panel devices) are frequently accompanied by an INIT.

A CDEV is a small program which enables you to set system options for memory-handling, monitor display, and so on. CDEVs are also sometimes paired with an extension, so that you can set options for the extension. To select and use a CDEV, you open the Control Panel or Control Panels desk accessory.

Selecting and Installing System Software

QUESTION: What is the "right" version of system software for my Mac?

ANSWER: See Figure 2.1, the *Compatible System Software* chart, for supported, recommended, and required versions of system software for all Macs.

Many Mac owners seem to think that the version of system software that comes with their Mac is the one they should stay with forever. Not so. Anyone who owns a Plus or higher should now be running a version of System 6 or 7, for example. Maintaining compatibility with current programs should be enough by itself to convince most users of the need to upgrade. Almost all programs now require you to use System 6.0.4 or higher to work correctly.

The *Compatible System Software* chart in Figure 2.1 summarizes Apple's system software recommendations as of August, 1992. A "required" symbol indicates that no earlier version of system software will work with that particular Mac. (Usually, you can assume that *later* versions of the system software will also work.)

The difference between a "recommended" and "supported" (OK to use) version of system software is that the recommended version will provide your Mac with all the features of that major revision. As an example, System 7.0 is recommended for older Macs in the chart.

Although they can also run System 7.0.1 (a supported version), no new features or functionality will be gained by doing so.

Compatible System Software

Sys. Version	Macintosh Plus	Macintosh SE	Macintosh SE/30	Macintosh Classic	Macintosh Classic II	Macintosh II	Macintosh IIx
System 6.0.5	✔	✔	✔			✔	✔
System 6.0.7	✔	✔	✔	✔		✔	✔
System 6.0.8	✔	✔	✔	✔		✔	✔
System 7.0*	☆	☆	☆	☆		☆	☆
System 7.0.1*	✔	✔	✔	✔	☆	✔	✔

Sys. Version	Macintosh IIcx	Macintosh IIci	Macintosh IIfx	Macintosh IIsi	Macintosh LC	Macintosh LC II	Macintosh Portable
System 6.0.5	✔	✔	✔				✔
System 6.0.7	✔	✔	✔	✔	✔		✔
System 6.0.8	✔	✔	✔	✔	✔	✔	✔
System 7.0*	☆	☆	☆	☆	☆	☆	☆
System 7.0.1*	✔	✔	✔	✔	✔	✔	✔

Sys. Version	Macintosh Quadra 700	Macintosh Quadra 900	Macintosh Quadra 950	Macintosh PowerBook 100	Macintosh PowerBook 140	Macintosh PowerBook 145	Macintosh PowerBook 170
System 6.0.5							
System 6.0.7							
System 6.0.8							
System 7.0*							
System 7.0.1*	☆	☆	☆	☆	☆	☆	☆

✔ OK to use
☆ Recommended

If you are using either System 7.0 or 7.0.1, it is recommended that you also install the most recent System 7 Tune-Up.

QUESTION: When is it necessary to upgrade to a new version of system software?

ANSWER: The time to upgrade is when you want or need the features offered by the new version, or to be compatible with new programs.

Figure 2.1

Compatible System Software.

There are several reasons that Apple introduces new versions of system software. They include:

- the introduction of new features or improved operation,

- support for new Macs, and

- corrections for problems or "bugs" in the previous version.

Determining whether you can or should upgrade to a new version is often confusing. One important reason to upgrade is if you have an essential program that only runs with the new system software. For example, Apple's QuickTime extension (which enables you to display movies inside of many kinds of documents) requires System 6.0.7 or higher.

Another common reason for upgrading is "feature lust." If you want to use balloon help, virtual memory, aliases, stationery pads, or Publish & Subscribe, you *must* upgrade to System 7.

QUESTION: Rather than go through the process of using the Installer program to install (or reinstall) system software, can't I just copy the new System and Finder to my hard disk?

ANSWER: In general, this isn't a good idea. Before System 6 was introduced, this was an accepted (and easy) method for installing or updating system software on your disks. Now, however, there are so many components that must be updated that this procedure is likely to result in errors. Using the Installer program that comes with each set of system software assures that you won't end up with a mix-and-match system (some current system software components and some older, outdated ones). Also, installers know what the right parts are for your particular Mac.

The System Software Upgrade Blues

PROBLEM: I've recently upgraded my Mac to a new version of system software, and now my hard disk, monitor, etc., no longer work properly.

SOLUTION: The hardware's *device driver* software may not be compatible with the new system software. Contact the hardware manufacturer for a revised version of their software.

Until you receive the new driver, you will either not be able to use that particular piece of hardware, or you should reinstall the old system software that you were using before you upgraded.

PROBLEM: I've recently upgraded my Mac to a new version of system software, and some of my programs no longer work properly.

SOLUTION #1: This is frequently a problem when a major system software revision is released (going from System 6 to System 7, for example). Minor upgrades (between 7.0 and 7.0.1, for instance) are generally less problematic. Contact the software publisher to see if an upgrade or fix is available.

SOLUTION #2: Reinstall the old system software. If the problems occur in a program which is critical to your business, reverting to the older system software may be unavoidable. (You'll have to do this while waiting for a fix, anyway.) If a compatible version of the program is not planned (the manufacturer has abandoned the program, for instance), you will either have to begin looking for a new program, or keep that particular Mac "frozen in time" restricting it to the older system software.

SOLUTION #3: Before upgrading to a new version of system software, you should consider two utilities (Compatibility Checker and Help!) that can help determine the extent of the compatibility problems you are likely to encounter. If you are thinking about upgrading to System 7, the System 7 distribution disks include a HyperCard stack called Compatibility Checker. When you run this stack by double-clicking it, it scans all the drives attached to your system, and compiles a list of what it finds (all programs, DAs, and so on). Compatibility Checker will note any known compatibility problems and will remove any INITs that are no longer needed when running System 7.

NOTE

If you're new to HyperCard, see the HyperCard instruction manual that came with your Mac. You must install the HyperCard program before running any of the HyperCard stacks.

One of the functions of Help!, a commercial program by Teknosys, is to scan all drives and look for compatibility problems specific to the system software. It can be used to check for compatibility problems with any version of system software—not just System 7. Both utilities work from a database of manufacturers' compatibility statements. Of the two, Help!'s database is much more complete and up-to-date.

System 7: Features and Issues

PROBLEM: I'm trying to choose menu commands or select dialog box options, but a tiny "thought balloon" keeps popping up instead.

SOLUTION: Turn off Balloon Help. *Balloon Help* is a feature of System 7 that displays pop-up "thought balloons" whenever you move the cursor over an object on the desktop or in a program that has associated help information. Balloon Help can be turned off or on by selecting the appropriate command from the Balloon Help menu (found under the balloon icon in the upper right corner of the screen).

QUESTION: What's an "alias?"

ANSWER: It's a stand-in for a document, program, folder, or disk. Aliases are one of the handiest features of System 7. By selecting a file, folder, or disk icon and making an alias from it (select **Make Alias** from the desktop's **File** menu), you can use the alias to refer to the original file, folder, or disk that it represents. Double-click an alias and it does exactly what the original icon did. If it's a folder, it opens and displays the real folder for you. If it's a program icon, the real program is launched. Unlike the original document it represents, an alias uses only a little disk space. Since they're tiny, you should feel free to make as many as you need.

As example, you might make aliases of frequently used programs, files, or folders, and place them along the bottom edge of your screen. Rather than hunt for them each time they're needed, you can keep them out in the open and accessible. You may also find it useful to place aliases in the Apple Menu Items folder inside of the System Folder. Doing this adds them to the Apple menu along with your desk accessories. This is another good spot for your favorite programs, important CDEVs (control panel devices or documents), and current project files.

When aliases no longer serve a function (you've finished a project, for instance, so you no longer need aliases of the important files), just drag the aliases to the Trash.

PROBLEM: I need to run some very large programs but don't have enough memory.

SOLUTION: You can use your hard disk as *virtual memory* to supplement your normal RAM.

By turning virtual memory on (in the Memory control panel), selecting a hard disk, and specifying the amount of space to use, you instruct the Mac to use hard disk space as supplemental memory. Your Mac must contain a *PMMU* (Paged Memory Management Unit) chip for virtual memory to be presented as an option for you. See your owner's manual if you aren't sure whether your Mac contains a PMMU chip.

▼ TIP

Most users should treat virtual memory as a "once in a while" thing, rather than as a standard operating mode. Sometimes, for instance, you may find that you just have to run two or three large programs at the same time. Because disk-based memory is incredibly slow when compared to RAM, you won't be happy if you have to use virtual memory all the time. (If you find yourself in this situation, it's definitely time to consider adding more RAM to your Mac.)

PROBLEM: I've just upgraded to System 7, and my Mac seems a lot slower than it was under System 6.

SOLUTION #1: Be sure that you have also installed the latest version of System 7 Tune-Up. Tune-Up helps improve System 7 performance.

SOLUTION #2: Try increasing the Cache Size setting for the disk cache in the Memory control panel (refer to Figure 2.2). The Cache Size setting is the amount of RAM (memory) that is used to supplement your hard disk(s). As data is read from a hard disk, the cache stores portions of it in high-speed RAM. The next time data is needed, the cache is checked first to see if the data is there. If it is, the data is grabbed directly from the cache rather than your hard disk—which is much slower than RAM. Every time data is found in the cache (this is called a "hit"), you save a little time. And, or course, the larger the disk cache, the more likely that the needed data will be found there.

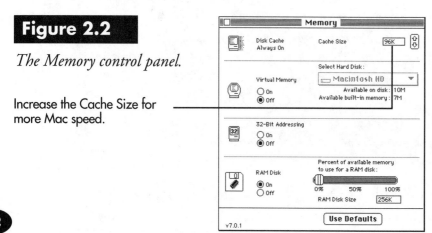

Figure 2.2

The Memory control panel.

Increase the Cache Size for
more Mac speed.

How Many System Folders Is Too Many? (and Other System Folder Mysteries)

You should never have more than one System Folder on any disk. And unless you intend to boot the Mac from the disk in question, you don't need a System Folder on it at all.

Having multiple System Folders on the same disk can cause all sorts of horrendous problems—including messages that a font can't be found (or the wrong font being displayed), programs that no longer run, printing difficulties, and crashes.

NOTE

A crash is an event in which the Mac is brought to its knees—that is, it stops running. A number of occurrences may accompany a crash. The cursor may freeze on-screen, and keyboard input may be ignored. A dialog box containing a picture of a bomb may appear. Sometimes, the screen will be filled with ugly lines, and horrible static will be emitted from the Mac's speaker. Although not dangerous to your hardware, a crash may be injurious to your data. You will not be able to save documents that were open when the Mac crashed. In most cases, the only thing you can do when the Mac crashes is to reboot and assess the damage.

The system software inside the System Folder is responsible for making your Mac and its peripherals operate smoothly. If you have more than one System Folder on your startup disk, the Mac may become confused and think that the *other* System Folder is the one that should be used. Since fonts and desk accessories that are in your main System Folder may not be present in the other System Folders, the Mac is liable to (figuratively) toss its hands in the air or shoot itself in the head.

The most common way to end up with multiple System Folders is by copying entire program disks to your hard disk. Some of these disks will contain their own System Folder. If you suspect that you have multiple System Folders, use System 7's **Find** command (in the **File** menu), or System 6's **Find File** desk accessory to search for "Finder" or "System." If more than one Finder or System file is found, drag the extra System Folder(s) to the Trash.

QUESTION: There are several new files in the System Folder that I didn't create. Is it safe to get rid of them?

ANSWER: Only if you know what they are and what they do. When you install a program, run it for the first time, or save preferences, many programs store their preferences data, help files, and other important files inside the System Folder. If you're lucky, the program will name the file in a manner that makes it easy for you to associate it with the creating program. Dragging any of these files to the Trash may make the program stop running or display an error message when you choose certain program functions.

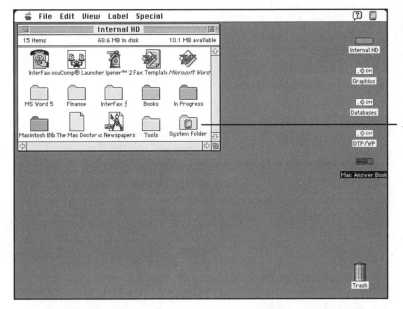

Figure 2.3

The System Folder is at the root level of your startup disk.

System folder

In general, the only new files of this sort that can safely be removed are those you are certain are associated with a particular program that has been removed from your system. If you switch to a different spreadsheet program, for instance, you can throw away any files associated with the older program.

System software components you don't use can often be removed as well. Not only can you save a little disk space, you may also reduce the memory requirements of the system software in the process. See "The System Software Upgrade Blues" later in this chapter for suggestions on files that can be eliminated.

Startup Problems

QUESTION: I have a hard disk. How can I make the Mac start up from a floppy?

ANSWER: During the boot sequence, insert a floppy that contains a valid System Folder on it.

When starting up, the Mac checks all attached drives for a valid *boot disk*. (A boot disk is any floppy or hard disk that contains a valid or "blessed" System Folder—a System Folder with a tiny Mac icon on it.) As such, the disk has been certified by the Mac as being able to boot or start up the Mac.) The check for a boot disk is performed in the following order: internal floppy drive, external floppy drive(s), the user-specified startup drive, and all other drives. As long as the floppy is inserted before the Mac has a chance to check your hard disk, the floppy will be used to boot the system.

PROBLEM: I've just started up my Mac, and it's showing me a disk icon with an 'X' through it.

SOLUTION: The current disk does not contain a valid System Folder, or critical files in the System folder may be damaged. In either case, it is not considered a startup disk.

This happens most often when you're trying to start up the Mac by inserting a floppy disk. If the Mac doesn't find a valid System Folder on the disk, it will eject it and display this icon. To correct the problem, insert a disk that has a System Folder, such as the Disk Tools disk from the system software.

TIP

Disks and the files they contain can occasionally become damaged. For this reason, it's safer to work from copies of program disks than to work from the originals. Protect your investment in a program by safely stashing the master disks somewhere else. If your working copy becomes damaged, you can always make a fresh copy from the master. (Note, however, that some installation routines only work from the original disks, not copies. See your program manuals for instructions.)

PROBLEM: I've just turned on my Mac, and it's showing me a disk with a question mark on it.

SOLUTION: The Mac can't find a startup disk (one with a valid System Folder on it).

Under System 7, you must specify a startup disk in the Startup Disk control panel. Although this is automatically done for you when you install or reinstall System 7, the Mac can sometimes lose track of your selection. To set a startup disk:

1. Select **Control Panels** from the **Apple** menu. Your Control Panels folder will open.

2. Double-click the **Startup Disk** icon. The Startup Disk control panel will be displayed (see Figure 2.4).

Figure 2.4

The Startup Disk control panel (System 7).

3. Click once to select the disk that contains your System Folder; that is, the one you always want the Mac to start up from.

4. Close the **Startup Disk** control panel window.

If you are running System 6 and have an SE, II, or newer Mac, there is a similar control panel called Startup Device that you can use to select a startup disk. Earlier Macs, such as the Plus, cannot designate a particular startup disk. The default scanning order is used instead.

PROBLEM: I've just turned on my Mac, and I hear a funny-sounding chord or see a Sad Mac face.

SOLUTION #1: There may be something wrong with the Mac's RAM (memory) chips, logic board, or another critical piece of hardware.

At startup, the Mac performs some general diagnostics to determine if it is ready to run. Normally, you'll hear a pleasant chord that indicates that everything is hunky-dory. An odd chord, on the other hand, suggests that there's something seriously wrong, such as a bank of RAM that is not functioning properly. Take your Mac for a visit to the repair shop. (Before doing that, you may want to make sure that your NuBus cards and memory are firmly in place. Push down on the parts.)

SOLUTION #2: If this happens on selecting Restart following a crash, the Mac may be so scrambled that it hasn't been able to reset itself properly. Turn off all power to the Mac and its peripherals. After a reasonable period of time (a few minutes is usually sufficient), turn the power back on and boot the Mac. If this fails to correct the problem, contact your dealer or an Apple repair service.

SOLUTION #3: If this occurs immediately after you've installed new RAM, the RAM *SIMMs* (single in-line memory modules) are probably installed incorrectly or are not seated properly. Check the installation instructions to see that each SIMM is in the correct bank (set of slots); reinsert the SIMMs, if necessary. If there is no change after rebooting, contact the company from whom you purchased the RAM for further instructions.

PROBLEM: My Mac is crashing during the startup sequence; it is unable to get as far as displaying the normal desktop and may display an error message or a picture of a bomb.

SOLUTION: You probably have an INIT/extension conflict or one of the INITs may be damaged.

If you have an extension management utility (discussed later in this chapter), attempt to reboot the Mac while pressing the appropriate key to disable all extensions. If you are running System 7, you can accomplish this without an extension manager by holding down the **Shift** key as you reboot.

If you do not have an extension management utility and are running System 6, you'll have to boot the Mac from a floppy disk. Insert a floppy that contains a legitimate System Folder (you can use the Disk Tools disk that comes with the system software), and then restart the Mac.

Once you have successfully booted the Mac, refer to the INIT/extension troubleshooting tips later in this chapter for help in identifying the trouble-maker(s).

Other System Problems

QUESTION: What is "rebuilding the desktop?"

ANSWER: Every disk has either one or two invisible desktop files on it (one file under System 6, two under System 7). The desktop keeps track of windows and their positions, and the names and locations of every file and folder. As you make changes, the system software updates the desktop file(s) to track those changes.

As time passes, the desktop file(s) grow. Part of this expansion is because they also keep track of files that are no longer on the disk; that is, files that you have dragged to the Trash and deleted. Rebuilding the desktop causes the system software to recreate the desktop file(s) from scratch and allows them to discard irrelevant and out-of-date information about the disk and its contents.

To rebuild the desktop, hold down ⌘-**Option** while booting the Mac. For each disk attached to the Mac, you will be asked whether or not you wish to rebuild its desktop. As routine maintenance, you should periodically rebuild the desktop—once every month or two is usually sufficient.

PROBLEM: Files that I save have the wrong date or time.

SOLUTION #1: Reset the Mac's clock. In order to time- and date-stamp files correctly, the Mac's clock must be set for the right time and date. They can be set by opening the **General** control panel.

SOLUTION #2: Replace the battery. Every Mac has a battery that keeps the clock up-to-date while the system is off. If the battery is wearing out or has died, the clock may start keeping inaccurate track of time. See your user manual for battery replacement instructions.

PROBLEM: The Mac is losing track of my system software settings, such as the identity of the current startup disk and the system date.

SOLUTION: "Zap the PRAM (parameter RAM)." System software settings are recorded in a special bank of memory referred to as the *PRAM*. If these settings become corrupted, it is necessary to "zap the PRAM," wiping it clean.

If you have a Mac Plus or older system, the way to zap the PRAM is to shut down the Mac, remove its battery, and then wait approximately half an hour before replacing it.

To zap the PRAM on a newer Mac running System 6:

1. Hold down the ⌘, **Shift**, and **Option** keys while selecting the **Control Panel** desk accessory from the **Apple** menu.

2. Respond in the affirmative to the dialog box, and the PRAM will be reset.

To zap the PRAM in System 7, hold down ⌘-**Shift-P-R** while booting the Mac. Unlike System 6, you will not see a dialog box asking if you want to zap the PRAM, nor will you receive a message stating that the action has been carried out. The only way you can tell the PRAM has been zapped is that open windows and startup items won't be present.

Regardless of the method you use to zap the PRAM, after restarting your Mac you should confirm that the correct startup disk has been chosen and reset the date and time in the General control panel. If the Mac continues to lose track of these settings, it may be indicative of a failing battery. See your user manual for battery replacement instructions.

PROBLEM: My Mac keeps crashing or the cursor freezes. (Other symptoms of a crash can include a garbled screen and noisy static from the speaker, or a dialog box with the picture of a bomb in it.)

SOLUTION #1: You may have bumped into a software bug or incompatibility. If you notice that this always happens when you're running a particular program or desk accessory, or if it always occurs when you perform a particular set of actions, you may have discovered a program bug or software incompatibility. See Chapter 8 for some suggestions for rooting out the culprit(s).

SOLUTION #2: Part of the system software may be corrupted and should be replaced. When your Mac crashes, garbage data will sometimes be written into parts of the system software. In future sessions, when a program needs specific system data (called *resources*), it tries to read them from the system software. If the needed resources are now garbled, it can cause the program—and the Mac—to crash. Unfortunately, there is no reliable way to determine if your system software is corrupted. Frequent crashes, though, are often a symptom.

If resources have been corrupted, using the Installer to reinstall the system software into the existing System Folder can occasionally fail to correct the corruption. The best way to make certain you end up with a clean version of the system software is to get rid of the current system software entirely—and then reinstall a clean copy, as follows:

Reinstalling System 6

1. Run **Font/DA Mover**, and use it to make new suitcase files that contain all the non-Apple fonts and desk accessories that are currently installed in the System file. As an alternative, you can copy the System file to a different disk.

2. Restart the Mac from a floppy disk that contains a System Folder. If you don't have a separate disk for this purpose, you can use the disk in the system software set that contains the disk tools.

3. Open the **System Folder** on your hard disk, and throw the **System** and **Finder** into the **Trash**.

4. Restart the Mac with Installer Disk 1 from the system software. Reinstall the system software onto your hard disk.

5. Use **Font/DA Mover** to reinstall the non-Apple fonts and desk accessories into the new System file.

6. Select **Chooser** from the **Apple** menu, and select your printer.

Reinstalling System 7

1. Use the **Finder** to make copies of all non-Apple fonts and sounds that are currently installed in the System file. (Double-click the **System** file to open it, and then copy the non-Apple font and sound resources using normal Finder copy procedures.) As an alternative, you can copy the System file to another disk.

2. Restart the Mac from a floppy disk that contains a System Folder. If you don't have a separate disk for this purpose, you can use the Disk Tools disk from the system software.

3. Open the **System Folder** on your hard disk, and throw the **System** and **Finder** into the **Trash**.

4. Restart the Mac with Installer Disk 1 from the system software. Reinstall the system software onto your hard disk. (You may be

notified that you are about to replace newer versions of some files with older ones. Click the **Continue** button to proceed.)

5. Install the latest version of System 7 Tune-Up. The older resources installed in the previous step will now be brought up-to-date.

6. Use standard Finder copy procedures to reinstall the non-Apple fonts and sounds into the new System file. (Drag the fonts and sounds onto the new System file icon.)

7. Select **Chooser** from the **Apple** menu, and select your printer.

TIP

Following these steps is also the best way to upgrade to a new version of system software as well.

SOLUTION #3: You may have an INIT conflict.

Problems can arise when one INIT conflicts with another or with one of your programs. A variety of bizarre problems can occur when an INIT conflict is present, including system crashes and freezes. To determine if you have an INIT conflict, do the following:

• Restart the Mac with all INITs turned off. (See Chapter 1 for instructions for doing this.) See if the problem reoccurs. If it does, the problem is obviously caused by something other than an INIT conflict.

- If you cannot reproduce the problem after the INITs have been turned off, it may very well be an INIT conflict. You will have to track down the conflicting INIT and remove it. Start by looking for pairs of INITs that perform the same or a similar function— two appointment alarm INITs, for example. Remove one of them and see if the problem disappears.

- If you can't find any common pairs, turn the INITs back on one at a time, rebooting the system each time. When the problem appears again, the last INIT turned on is the likely culprit.

TIP

Regardless of the version of system software installed on your Mac, you may find it easier to handle INITs with an extension manager. Extension managers allow you to selectively turn INITs on and off without moving them out of the System Folder. Many of these utilities also let you define groups of extensions. Since I don't use it very often, for instance, I've defined my default group of extensions to exclude the QuickTime extension. Some popular extension managers include INITPicker (Microseeds), StartUp Manager (part of the NOW Utilities from NOW Software), and Extension Manager (a freeware utility programmed by Apple Computer).

- Occasionally, the *order* in which INITs load can be the cause of the problem. Since they load alphabetically, you can modify the loading order by renaming them or by changing the order in your extension manager, if it offers this feature. Note, however, that some INITs may not run properly if they have been renamed.

- If you identify the conflict (or have given up), call the software publisher(s) for assistance. If all of your problems occur when running a particular program, the publisher of that program may be able to identify the problematic INIT for you.

PROBLEM: My Mac has crashed or locked up. What do I do now?

SOLUTION #1: If a system bomb is *not* displayed, you can try these steps:

1. If the keyboard is not locked, you may be able to save any open documents before rebooting the Mac. Try pressing ⌘-**S** (to save) and ⌘-**Q** to quit the current program. If you're successful, you won't lose your work in progress.

2. Press ⌘-**.** (period). This is a universal stop or cancel command. If the current program isn't dead, it may respond and allow you to save your files and quit normally.

3. Issue the emergency quit command (⌘-**Option-Esc**). If it works, you will lose any unsaved changes to the current document(s), but you may be able to regain control of the Mac long enough to gracefully exit from other open programs.

4. If possible, return to the desktop and attempt to select the **Shut Down** command from the **Special** menu. This will allow the Mac to note changes to the desktop and finish any necessary writing to your hard disk before shutting down the system.

5. If these steps fail, you'll have little choice other than to reboot by whatever means possible. Rather than simply shutting off the power, it's preferable to hit the Mac's **Reset** button (if so equipped), or use the programmer's switch (if one was included with your Mac and you installed it).

CAUTION

If you manage to regain control of the Mac following a system error, you should immediately save all open documents (under new names, if possible, in case they've been damaged), quit from all programs, and shut down the Mac. Wait for a minute or so, turn the power back on, and reboot.

SOLUTION #2: If the Mac *is* displaying a system bomb dialog box, *there is no practical way to recover.* Changes made to any open documents will be lost. Click the **Restart** button, or reboot the Mac by pressing its **Reset** button or the programmer's switch.

After a serious error, there's no telling how confused the Mac may be. Rather than risk damaging your files, it's preferable to err on the side of caution by rebooting. You should also run any hard disk diagnostic programs that you have following a crash. There may be errors in your directory, for example, that should be corrected.

Memory Issues

PROBLEM: I'm running System 6 and have a lot of INITs, desk accessories, and fonts installed. My Mac crashes frequently.

SOLUTION: It's likely that you are running out of system *heap space*, a special area of the Mac's RAM that is reserved for system software functions. The solution is to increase the system *heap space*.

When you select **About the Finder...** from the **Apple** menu, you'll see a window like the one in Figure 2.5. The System bar is the important one. The black area of the bar represents memory that is currently in use. The lighter colored area represents free memory. To avoid heap problems, you should normally have 20–30 percent of the memory in the System bar free at startup. In a bare-bones system with few demands on the system heap (no extra fonts and few DAs and INITs), achieving this objective is easy. As you add more fonts, DAs, and INITs, however, you're likely to encounter heap-related problems.

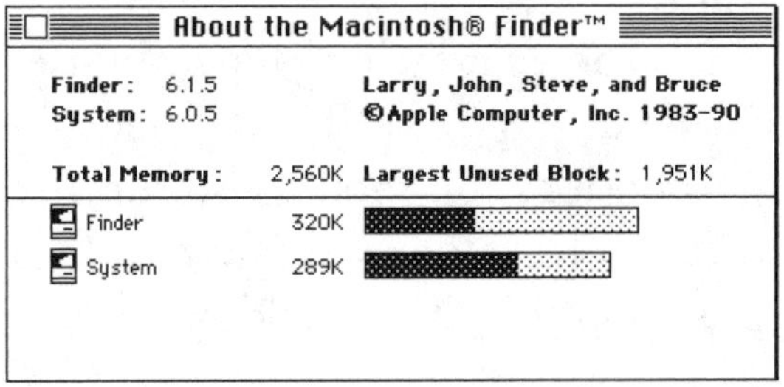

Figure 2.5

The About the Macintosh Finder... window.

Finder:	6.1.5		Larry, John, Steve, and Bruce	
System:	6.0.5		©Apple Computer, Inc. 1983–90	
Total Memory:		2,560K	Largest Unused Block:	1,951K
Finder		320K		
System		289K		

About the Macintosh® Finder™

Unfortunately, Apple did not (and does not) provide a way for users to adjust the heap space. Whether Apple thought this was beyond most users (or didn't foresee the "maxed-out" systems that many of us would create) is irrelevant. The question is: *What can we do about it?* There are three solutions.

SOLUTION #1: Use a heap adjustment utility. Two popular heap adjusters are Heap Fixer and HeapTool. The former is a standalone program included with many of the utilities from CE Software. If your system is fairly static, Heap Fixer is a good solution. You run it, tell Heap Fixer how much space you want to allocate to the system heap, and then reboot for the changes to take effect. If, on the other hand, you change your system configuration on a frequent basis—adding or removing DAs and INITs, for example—Heap Fixer's approach is far from optimal. As your heap needs change, you'll have to re-run Heap Fixer.

HeapTool is a shareware INIT/CDEV (control panel device) combination that is ideal for people who frequently monkey with their system. Rather than assign a fixed amount of heap space as Heap Fixer does, HeapTool lets you specify the amount of free space that you want it to maintain *beyond the heap space required at startup.* Thus, whether you add or remove DAs and INITs, the amount of heap space is adjusted automatically each time you boot the Mac.

NOTE

A program that is shareware can be freely copied and given to others. If, after using the program, you decide to keep it, you send a contribution or recommended fee to the author of the program. Freeware programs, on the other hand, cost nothing at all. Both shareware and freeware programs can be obtained by modem from BBSs and information services (such as Prodigy, America Online, and CompuServe), from user groups, and from companies that publish shareware/ freeware catalogs, such as Educorp (800/843-9497).

SOLUTION #2: Remove unnecessary INITs, DAs, and fonts. Then reboot the Mac and see whether these changes have had the necessary impact on the system heap by checking **About the Finder...** again.

SOLUTION #3: Install System 7. Heap space is dynamically adjusted by System 7. As new software is called into play, System 7 increases the system heap automatically to accommodate the demands made on it. Theoretically, you should never see a heap problem. (Personally, however, I'm not convinced that they're gone for good. On my packed system, About This Macintosh... frequently shows almost no free heap space.)

PROBLEM: I just increased my Mac's memory to more than 8M. Why will it still only let me use 8M?

SOLUTION: Install System 7, and turn on 32-bit addressing in the Memory control panel.

Prior to System 7, the system software would only support up to 8M of RAM, regardless of how much was installed in the Mac. Under System 7, the Mac can address additional RAM above 8M only if you turn on **32-bit addressing** in the **Memory** control panel.

CAUTION

Not all programs are compatible with 32-bit addressing. If you find ones that are incompatible (that is, they crash frequently), you should contact the software publisher for information about a possible fix or a new version.

You should note that not all Macs can support 32-bit addressing. To use 32-bit addressing, the Mac II, IIx, IIcx, and SE/30 need a System 7 extension called MODE32, available free from most information services and user groups.

PROBLEM: I can't create a RAM disk.

SOLUTION: Depending on your model of Macintosh, System 7.0.1 may include a RAM disk option in the Memory control panel. A RAM disk works like any real floppy or hard disk, except that it's created from the memory in your computer. You can copy and save files to a RAM disk, as well as launch programs from it. Since it uses memory to create the disk, accessing the disk (loading files from it or saving files to it) happens almost instantaneously.

CAUTION

On most Macs, the entire contents of the RAM disk will disappear automatically when the Mac is shut down. If the RAM disk contains important data files that you want to preserve, be certain to copy them to another disk before shutting down.

System 7.0.1 offers RAM disk support for the following Macintosh models *only*: PowerBooks, Quadras, and the Macintosh Portable. Users of other Mac models must use a shareware, public domain, or commercial utility program if they need to set up a RAM disk.

To set up a RAM disk for a supported Mac under System 7.0.1:

1. Select the **Control Panels** DA from the **Apple** menu.

2. Double-click the **Memory** control panel icon to open the control panel (see Figure 2.2).

3. Click the **On** button for the **RAM Disk** portion of the control panel, and use the slider control to specify the amount of RAM to allocate to the RAM disk.

4. Restart your Mac. The RAM disk will appear on your desktop.

PROBLEM: I've just upgraded to System 7 and seem to be running out of memory.

SOLUTION: Compared to System 6, the new system software uses a lot more memory. Two steps you can take to reduce its memory requirements include the following:

- Get rid of extensions you don't need (it's worth repeating). On my system (a standalone Mac) these include AppleShare, DAL, File SharingExtension, and the Network Extension. Check through your Extension folder inside the System Folder for other extensions you never use, and then delete them or move them to a different folder (I call mine "Unused INITs"). If you later find that you need them, you can always drag the extensions back into the Extensions folder.

- Turn off **File Sharing** (with the **Sharing Setup** control panel) and **Virtual Memory** (with the **Memory** control panel) if you aren't using them.

TIP

*If you're really in a crunch, hold down the **Shift** key when you start up the Mac. This instructs the system to turn off all extensions for the session. Check **About This Macintosh...** in the **Apple** menu both when you have all your extensions loaded and when none of them are loaded. The difference shown in the System Software bar will be the total memory savings you have achieved by shutting down your extensions.*

Making the System Software Work for You

PROBLEM: I always start each computing session by running a particular program. Is there a way to make this happen automatically?

SOLUTION: Yes, by specifying a *startup program*. Both System 6 and
System 7 support the concept of a startup program—one or more
programs or desk accessories that you want to launch automatically at startup.

With System 6, the procedure differs slightly, depending on whether
you are running under the Finder or MultiFinder.

Specifying a Startup Program Under Finder

1. Return to the **Finder Desktop** and click once on a program to
   select it.

2. Select **Set Startup...** from the **Special** menu.

3. In the dialog box that appears (see Figure 2.6), set the Mac to
   open the selected program automatically.

Specifying a Startup Program Under MultiFinder

1. Return to the **Finder Desktop** and launch *each* program you
   want to open at startup (MultiFinder allows you to have multiple

programs open at the same time). If you also want to run one or more desk accessories at startup, open them now.

2. Select **Set Startup...** from the **Special** menu.

3. In the dialog box that appears, set the Mac to open the selected programs and DAs automatically.

Under System 7, you specify startup programs by dragging them into the **Startup Items** folder inside the System Folder.

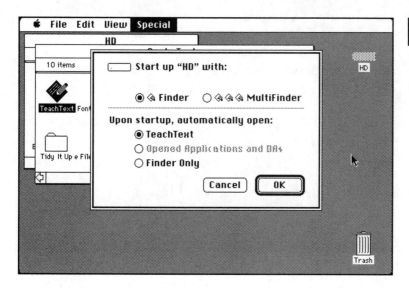

Figure 2.6

The Set Startup dialog box (System 6).

TIP

Rather than place the actual programs or DAs into the Startup Items folder, you can place aliases of those applications into the folder, as follows:

1. *Select the program or DA that you want to make into a startup item by clicking on it.*

2. *Select **Make Alias** from the Finder's **File** menu.*

3. *Drag the alias into the **Startup Items** folder.*

PROBLEM: I'm bored with the standard gray desktop. How can I change it?

SOLUTION: The General control panel lets you select or create new desktop patterns. See your Macintosh owner's manual for instructions.

PROBLEM: My desktop is filled with windows. How do I get rid of them?

SOLUTION #1: Clicking a window's close box (see Figure 2.7) will close the current window in the Finder. If you hold down the **Option** key while clicking a close box, the Mac will close *all* open Finder windows.

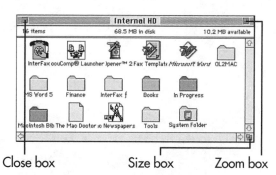

Figure 2.7

Windows may contain none, some, or all of these three boxes: close, zoom, and grow.

Close box   Size box   Zoom box

SOLUTION #2: If you're running System 7, you can get rid of window clutter temporarily by selecting **Hide Others** from the pull-down application menu in the right-hand corner of the screen (see Figure 2.8). Selecting this command removes all windows except those currently in use. If you are running WordPerfect, for example, the windows for all other programs will be hidden.

Figure 2.8

Various Hide commands appear in the application menu.

Selecting the **Hide Others** command from the **Finder Desktop** will hide the windows of *all* programs. To make the windows reappear, select the individual program names from the **Application** menu, or select **Show All**.

TIP

Some programs, such as spreadsheets, may have their own commands to help you arrange the windows of open documents aesthetically.

PROBLEM: How do I change the size of a window?

SOLUTION: Every resizable window—whether for a document or an open file folder—can be resized in one of two ways: using the window's *size box* or its *zoom box* (refer to Figure 2.7).

You use the *size box* to manually change the size of a window. Click in the size box and, while holding down the mouse button, drag until the window is the desired size. Click the *zoom box* to toggle a window between its maximum predefined size and its current size.

You can use the size and zoom boxes to manage multiple documents easily within a program. Suppose, for example, that there are four worksheets you need to use in your spreadsheet program. After opening all four, use the size box to shrink each worksheet to its smallest possible size. Then drag them to the bottom or top of the screen—somewhere out of the way. Click the zoom box of the one you want to use first. It will grow to its original size and fill the screen. When you want to switch to another worksheet, click the zoom box of the current one. It will shrink again, and move back to the bottom of the screen (or wherever you placed it originally). Click the zoom box of the next worksheet, and it will expand to full size.

Not all windows can be resized. If the window does not contain a grow or a zoom box, its size has been permanently fixed by the programmer.

Avoiding Viruses

Much like viruses that infect humans, computer viruses can invade disks and damage your data. Computer viruses are programs or code segments that a malicious programmer has designed with the sole purpose of altering your Mac's behavior, changing its performance, or destroying data—*without your knowledge or consent.*

Depending on how it is written, a virus can alter a disk's desktop file, change important system software files, erase hard disks, display a "humorous" message and disappear, or attach itself to other programs and continue to spread.

Computer viruses spread through contact. If you slip an infected floppy into your drive and run a program from the disk, the virus can readily infect any other program that you run during the same session. Give the infected disk to a colleague, and *another* hard disk becomes infected.

One type of virus is known as a *Trojan Horse*: a seemingly useful program with a hidden agenda. The program is actually a virus launcher. Running the program activates the virus.

The amount of damage a particular virus can cause ranges widely. Some viruses are relatively benign (one might display a message on a given date and then erase itself); some cause catastrophic damage (erasing your hard disk or contaminating data files). Frequent system crashes, disappearing files, and programs that no longer run properly may be a sign of a virus infection.

The actual risk of becoming infected depends on your computing practices. Allowing other people to use your Mac and downloading files from electronic bulletin board systems are common virus sources. Occasionally, even disks for commercial programs may be infected—right out of the box. Safe computing techniques are discussed in the rest of this chapter.

PROBLEM: I think my hard disk is "infected." How do I tell if it has a virus? And how can I get rid of it?

SOLUTION: Install a virus-detection utility and run it regularly. A *virus-detection* utility can scan any or all disks attached to your Mac (floppies, too) and determine if any of your programs, system software, or the Mac desktop is infected. Such a utility will point out the infected components, but it is up to you to correct the problem—usually by installing clean copies of programs and/or reinstalling system software.

Some programs also include *virus-removal* functions. After detecting a virus, the utility may be able to take all or some of the steps needed to eradicate the virus, leaving you with a clean system.

Anti-virus utilities may be written as extensions, control panel devices, or programs. Those that include an extension as all or part of the utility (such as Rival from Microseeds Publishing and Virex from Microcom) can be set to scan each disk as it is mounted or inserted and check every program as it is launched. Since virus code needs to be executed before it can do any damage, these precautions are excellent ways to avoid contamination—without requiring any action on your part. Each of these utilities can also do a scan of all attached hard disks at your request.

Disinfectant—a standalone anti-virus program available free through user's groups and on-line information services—can also detect or eliminate viruses. Instead of running automatically like Virex and Rival, though, it must be launched like any other program.

What Steps Can I Take to Avoid Future Virus Contamination?

There are several precautions that can help.

- Perform a virus scan of every unknown floppy before copying its contents to your hard disk, or before running any programs from that floppy. Anyone else who will be using your Mac must be instructed to do the same. Although it's extremely rare, even disks from commercial programs may be infected. This is the best way to avoid problems!

- Do periodic virus scans of all attached hard disks. Unless you're working on a public Mac (shared by one or many other people), scanning once every couple of weeks should suffice.

- Use caution when acquiring new software. If not carefully policed by the system operator (SYSOP), bulletin board systems can be sources of infected programs. (Although just downloading the new software will not infect your Mac, *running* it will. Be sure to scan every downloaded file before executing it.)

- If your virus program offers a subscription update service, buy it. New viruses are introduced all the time. To maintain its effectiveness, your anti-virus software must be made aware of the new viruses, too.

Moving On

The next chapter examines disk-related problems and issues, including SCSI connections, hard disk maintenance, and floppy problems.

Problems with Disks

Other than seeing the Sad Mac face, disk-related problems are the ones of greatest concern to most users. A disk that has been damaged or has developed bad sectors can mean lost data—and time lost reconstructing the data. This chapter shows you how to handle the most common disk-related problems. Problems with *files* are covered in the next chapter.

Getting Organized

When they first get a Mac, many new users save all their files to the root (main) level of their hard disk. When you only have a couple of programs and a handful of files, this doesn't pose a problem. As your software collection expands and you create more data files, however, finding a particular program or file in this mess can be a chore. (And if your Mac is an office computer and you ever leave on vacation, imagine the difficulty your coworkers will have finding anything on your disk.)

TIP

The more files that the Finder sees at any particular level of your disk (this includes the root and within individual folders), the harder time it will have keeping track of them all. You'll see this especially when opening a packed folder. The more files it contains, the longer it will take to open.

To straighten out this mess, you can organize your programs and files within folders. (A folder is equivalent to a directory on a PC.) And you can nest folders within other folders as many layers deep as you need. To create a new folder:

1. Go to the desktop and click to select the disk on which the folder should be created.

2. Select **New Folder** from the **File** menu. A folder named "Empty Folder" (System 6) or "untitled folder" (System 7) is created for you.

Back to getting organized.... Folders allow you to categorize your programs and data, making it simpler to find whatever you need at the moment. How you organize your files and folders is up to you. Whatever makes sense and works for you is the right way to organize. If you're short on structure, though, here are a couple of approaches that can serve as a starting point for you.

The Ultra Simple Approach

Begin by making two folders at the root level of your hard disk, one named "Programs" and the other named "Data." Within the Programs folder, create a separate folder for each of your Mac programs, and store each program in its own folder. Within the Data folder, create new folders for each type of data you will be working with, such as Word Processing, Spreadsheets, Graphics, and Accounting. Whenever you save a file, use the Mac's File dialog box to direct it to the proper data folder. As these folders fill up, you may want to create additional subfolders, so you can group data files according to project, for example.

This approach (shown in Figure 3.1) makes it easy for colleagues and family members to find files if you aren't around. If a spreadsheet is desired, they (and you) will never have to look in more than one folder.

Organize by Program Type

As an alternative, you may find it simpler to organize entirely by program type (see Figure 3.2). At the root level of the hard disk, make a folder for each type of software you have: Word Processing, Graphics, Utilities, and so on. Within each of these

CAUTION

After creating a new folder, you should immediately give it a new name. Under System 6, other new folders will also be named Empty Folder, and there is a danger that you may lose the contents of the first Empty Folder. (If you create two folders with the same name, the second folder will replace the first folder—after a proper warning from the Mac.) Under System 7, if the Mac finds that you already have a folder called untitled folder, it tacks a number onto the end of other new folders to avoid a conflict (naming it "untitled folder 2," for example).

folders, make a new folder for each program of that type. In the Graphics folder, for example, you might have separate folders for Aldus SuperPaint, Adobe Illustrator, and MacDraw Pro. Now move (or install) your graphics programs into their respective folders. Inside each of the graphic program folders, you can create subfolders for each type of file (Business Clip Art) or for each project (1992 Annual Report).

Figure 3.1

Simple disk organization.

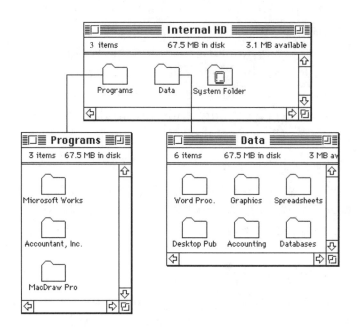

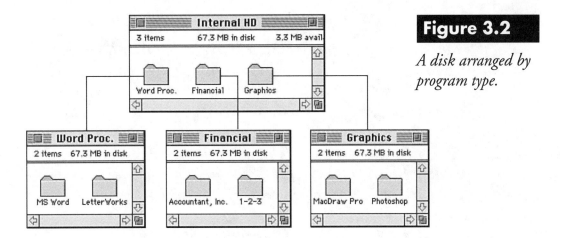

Figure 3.2

A disk arranged by program type.

Setting Up a Hard Disk (and Other SCSI Devices)

Hard disks and other SCSI devices are connected in series to the Mac's SCSI port. Other than hardware problems with the drives, four things can cause SCSI problems: the cables, the drive ID numbers, improper termination, and device order.

> *Throughout this chapter and at several points in this book, you'll see the phrase SCSI chain. SCSI devices, such as hard disks and scanners,*

continues

continued

can be connected to one another to form a chain. To understand how this works, imagine a toy train set with several box cars connected in a row behind the engine. In our computer setup, the Mac is the engine. The first car (an external hard disk, for example) is connected to the Mac's SCSI port by a cable. If you purchase another SCSI device, you can hook it to the external hard disk by plugging another SCSI cable into the hard disk's second SCSI port. You can continue linking additional SCSI devices into the chain until all the SCSI ID numbers (discussed below) have been used.

You'll note that most SCSI devices have two SCSI ports. This is what enables them to be chained together. One port is used to connect the device to the SCSI device ahead of it in the chain. The second port is used to hook up with the next device in the chain. For this reason, it's a bad idea to ever buy a SCSI device with only one port. By default, that device would have to be the final object in the SCSI chain, which could lead to hardware configuration problems.

Cable Problems

Damaged cables or connectors can cause SCSI problems. If you suspect a bad cable, a single good cable can be swapped in series for each of your other cables. When the problem disappears, you've found the cable that needs to be replaced. (The probability of two cables going bad at the same time is fairly small.)

Cable length can also be a problem. The maximum length of all SCSI cables should not exceed 20 feet.

ID Numbers

Each SCSI device must be assigned a unique SCSI ID number between 0 and 7. SCSI ID 7 is reserved for the Mac itself, and ID 0 is normally used for the internal hard disk, if you have one. All other devices in the SCSI chain must have a different ID number. ID numbers are usually set by manipulating tiny DIP switches, by turning a dial, or by pressing a button—all are generally mounted on the outside of the device. See your SCSI device manual for instructions.

Some devices are permanently wired for a particular SCSI ID. Never buy such a device. If you are unlucky and end up with two such devices that are both set for the same ID, you will have to sell, give, or throw one of them away. You cannot have two SCSI devices set for the same ID.

Improper Termination

To work correctly, the SCSI chain must be capped on each end; that is, the device closest to the Mac and the one furthest away in the chain must either contain a set of terminating resistors or have a terminating plug attached to one of its SCSI ports. Termination ensures that the signal sent down the SCSI chain bounces back to the Mac correctly.

The rule is that the first and last devices in the SCSI chain—and only these devices—must be terminated. Here are some common Mac set-ups and instructions for terminating each one correctly.

- Mac only: No problem. If the Mac has an internal hard disk, it is already terminated. If it doesn't have an internal hard disk, there are no SCSI devices to terminate.

- Mac with one external SCSI device: Terminate the external device. If the Mac also has an internal hard disk, it is already terminated.

- Mac with two or more external SCSI devices but no internal hard disk: Terminate the first and last devices in the chain.

- Mac with two or more external SCSI devices and an internal hard disk: Terminate only the final device in the chain. (The internal hard disk is already terminated.)

TIP

If your system won't recognize one or more devices in the chain,
- *make sure each device has a unique ID.*
- *make sure all devices are turned on.*
- *make sure the chain is properly terminated.*
- *make sure all cables are securely connected.*

If problems still persist:
- *try removing devices until things work.*
- *try moving the position of devices in the chain.*
- *try swapping cables.*

Also note that the IIfx requires a special black terminator—a normal gray one won't work! Most devices' internal termination is incompatible with fx SCSI, so you'll need to have it removed and use the black fx terminator.

Problems can arise if you don't know whether a particular device is internally terminated. Even if you ask the dealer or mail-order house to remove the terminators before shipping the drive to you, there's no way to be sure this has been done without opening the drive and checking it yourself. (See the device manual for help in locating the terminating resistors—they usually come in a set of three.)

As you buy new SCSI devices, you should immediately determine whether each one is internally terminated. If you have an internal hard disk, this means that only one new device can be terminated—the last one in the chain. Thus, you can leave the internal termination in one of the devices. If you don't have an internal hard disk, you can leave the internal termination in two of your external devices—using them as the first and last devices in the chain. You or someone else will have to take a pair of needle-nosed pliers and carefully yank out the terminating resistors in all of your other SCSI devices. Those devices must then be relegated to middle positions in the SCSI chain.

CAUTION

If needs dictate that the termination be restored to a device, don't try to reinsert the terminating resistors. It's far easier to buy a terminating plug from your dealer.

Device Order

According to their instruction manuals, some devices work better in a particular position in the SCSI chain—often requiring that they be first or last. If you aren't having any luck pinpointing a SCSI problem, try changing the order of the devices in the chain. Don't forget the termination rule, though.

Maintaining a Hard Disk

A driver is a piece of software that tells the Mac how to recognize and work with a particular hard disk. Most hard disks come with their own software for formatting, testing, and installing new drivers. You should use the Apple HD SC Setup program with hard disks that are sold by Apple, for example. In general, you should use the software that comes with each hard drive to install and update the driver for that hard disk. Installing or updating a driver is easily accomplished with most hard disk setup programs, and the process is nonthreatening to the data on the hard disk.

When Is It Necessary to Update the Driver for My Hard Disk?

You should update your driver whenever: you install a new version of system software, or you have encountered general hard disk problems that are unresolved by other troubleshooting approaches.

Like other software, drivers can become corrupted. Installing a clean driver will correct this. And when you install a new version of system software (particularly a major one such as the first release of System 6 or System 7), it is very important to update all hard disk drivers—if an update is available. When Apple ships new releases of the system software, they frequently include a new version of their HD SC Setup

CAUTION

If you have a third-party hard disk, you should not *use HD SC Setup unless instructed to do so by the manufacturer of your drive.*

program. After installing the system software, run HD SC Setup and click the Update button to install the new driver.

When switching to a new release of system software, you may find that the Mac refuses to recognize your third-party drive. Reinstalling the driver software may not correct the problem. In that case, you should contact the drive manufacturer about the availability of a new driver that is compatible with the system software.

If the manufacturer of your hard disk cannot or will not provide you with new driver software (they may have decided not to support the new system software or may have gone out of business), there is still a way to bring the driver up to date. Several software companies produce disk formatting, partitioning, and driver update software that is intended to work with almost any brand of hard disk. Two examples include Disk Manager Mac (Ontrack Computer Systems) and DiskMaker (Golden Triangle). Contact them to find out if your drive is supported before buying the software, however.

What Does It Mean to "Partition" a Hard Disk, and Why Would I Want to?

Partitioning a hard disk makes the Mac think that it is actually dealing with two or more separate hard disks instead of just one. You create the partitions by running a utility program.

HD SC Setup (a part of the system software) can be used to partition hard disks that are sold by Apple Computer. Other commercial utilities (such as DiskMaker from Golden Triangle), as well as some programs that are bundled with new hard drives (such as Disk Manager Mac), can be used to partition drives made by many manufacturers.

CAUTION

Creating partitions or changing their sizes will usually destroy all data on the disk. Be sure that you have a solid backup before proceeding.

In the partitioning process, you specify the number of partitions you want and the size each one should be. As an example, my 200M hard disk has been partitioned into three drives—each between 60 and 70M.

There are several advantages to partitioning a hard disk. The first is better organization. Each partition can be dedicated to a particular type of software and files (database programs, for instance) or to a particular project. Second, smaller drives are easier for the Finder to handle than larger ones. You may find that the Mac operates slightly quicker with several smaller drives than it does with one large one. Third, backing up is often more convenient with smaller drives. If you have a tape system with an 80M capacity, for example, it would take three tapes to back up a single 200M drive. If you partition the drive into three smaller units, you can do a full backup on each 80M tape, and still have room left over for several incremental backups.

Also, partitioning very large hard drives (larger than 120M) lets the system software make more efficient use of space. The smallest file will always occupy one allocation block, and for large hard drives an allocation block can be as large as 20 logical blocks. This means that a text file that contains one character will occupy a 10K chunk of disk space. If you have lots of small files, you're wasting space; large files aren't such a problem.

General Hard Disk Problems

PROBLEM: My hard disk is almost filled. What can I do to reclaim some disk space?

SOLUTION #1: Delete unneeded files. Just as most people occasionally go through their file cabinets and toss out old, outdated, and unneeded records, your hard disk also can benefit from a periodic housecleaning. Once a month or so, go through all the folders on your hard disk and toss out files you no longer need. Program tutorial files, for instance, are generally useless once you've worked through them.

SOLUTION #2: Compress seldom-used files. There are many utility programs that can compress files, making them take up less disk space than they originally used. This is a good solution for files that are only needed occasionally.

Compression utilities can be classified into two types: *manual* and *automatic*. The manual programs, such as StuffIt Deluxe, DiskDoubler, and Compact Pro, are standalone programs that must be launched like any other program. They can be used to compress files or folders and instructed to place the compressed files on any disk—including the original one. The original files can automatically be deleted by the compression program or left intact.

Compact Pro, a *shareware program* available for a small fee from user groups and information services, has an option that makes it very useful for archiving large numbers of files. After specifying the files and folders to be compressed, Compact Pro can automatically split the archive across a series of floppy disks. As each floppy fills, Compact Pro asks for another and continues until the archive is complete.

There are also several automatic compression utilities. AutoDoubler and More Disk Space both work in the background and compress entire hard disks! As files or programs are needed from the compressed disks, the utilities automatically decompress them. Unlike the manual compression utilities, you don't have to change your work habits to deal with compressed files. If you want to use a compressed word processing file and are using a *manual* compression program, you normally have to launch the compression program, decompress the file, and then return to your word processor before you can use the file. With an automatic program, all you have to do is launch your word processor and open the file normally. Decompression takes place automatically. Similarly, saving a file automatically marks it for compression.

Shortcut (a companion product to StuffIt Deluxe) provides one of the capabilities of the automatic compression utilities. It allows files to be compressed or decompressed from within any File dialog box (Open, Save, or Save As). When you save a file, for instance, you can use Shortcut to instruct StuffIt Deluxe to compress the file as it is saved. Similarly, any file that has been compressed by StuffIt Deluxe can be "unstuffed" from any Open dialog box.

SOLUTION #3: Archive seldom-used files. Just as you occasionally need to archive some business records, file *archiving* means to copy files to another disk and then delete the original files. Files are archive candidates when they are seldom used, but you feel that you might conceivably need them at some future time. Old accounting files are a good example of data that you may want to archive.

There are several ways to archive files. For small files, it's often easiest to just copy them to floppies and then drag the originals to the Trash.

If you use tape as your backup medium, you can put the month-end tape backup into storage, and use it as the basis for an archiving system. Finally, there are several backup programs that have built-in archiving capabilities—extremely useful when archiving large amounts of data. Both Retrospect and Fastback II can archive selected files and folders to almost any medium (tapes, floppies, and removable cartridge systems). The advantage of using either of these programs is that archiving is a one-step process. The selected files are copied and then automatically erased from the source drive.

SOLUTION #4: Rebuild the desktop. The system software automatically creates one or more invisible desktop files for each disk. These files contain a record of all the files and folders on that disk. As data and program files are deleted, however, the desktop files may continue to keep track of them—causing the desktop files to grow. The process of *rebuilding the desktop* compacts the desktop files, eliminating unneeded information about files that no longer exist. Depending on the length of time since you last rebuilt the desktop, you may be able to reclaim as much as several hundred kilobytes of disk space. To rebuild the desktop:

CAUTION

When archiving, it is extremely important that you verify that the archive is readable and is an exact copy of the original. If you are archiving by hand, be sure to try to open each archive file with its program before deleting the original file. If you are using a backup program to do the archiving, use the program's **Verify** *option to make sure that the backup was successful.*

1. Hold down the Option and ⌘ keys while booting the Mac.

2. You will be shown a dialog box that asks if you're sure that you want to rebuild the desktop. If you have multiple drives attached to your Mac, this dialog box will be repeated for each of the drives.

There is one negative aspect of rebuilding the desktop. If you have typed comments into any of the Get Info windows for files or programs on the selected disk (see Figure 3.3), those comments will be erased. If the comments are essential to you, there are alternate ways to rebuild the desktop that leave the comments intact, such as using Minor•Repairs (part of the 911 Utilities from Microcom).

Figure 3.3

Anything typed into a file or folder's Comments: box in the Get Info window is normally erased when rebuilding the desktop for the disk.

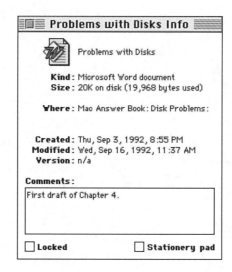

PROBLEM: It takes longer and longer to load and save files on my hard disk. What can I do to speed it up?

SOLUTION #1: Data on the drive has become fragmented. Run a defragmentation program. When a drive is newly formatted, programs and files that are copied or saved to the drive are normally kept together in contiguous chunks; that is, each file is written in one continuous string. However, when you make a new version of a file and save it over the original file, for example, there often isn't room to keep the file in one piece. A 25K data file can't fit in the same space previously occupied by an 18K file. To store that file, the system software may have to break it into pieces—placing part of it in one place and the remainder somewhere else on the disk. That file is now *fragmented*. Whenever you load the file, the disk drive now has to read it in two passes because it's no longer in one contiguous chunk.

Deleting files also creates holes on the disk. Over time, files will become increasingly fragmented. And as the disk gets close to being filled, fragmentation can get much worse. Some files—particularly large ones like the System file—may end up scattered in pieces all over your disk. And the more fragmented your files become, the longer it will take to read them or write new versions of them.

There are many commercial utilities for defragmenting disks. Most, such as those included in Central Point MacTools and Norton Utilities

CAUTION

Before using a defragmentation program, you should make sure that you have an up-to-date backup of the contents of that disk. In case anything goes wrong, you can always restore the data from the backup.

for the Mac, are manual programs that you run periodically. DiskExpress II from ALSoft is a background defragmentation utility that runs continuously.

 TIP

How often should you defragment a drive? One rule of thumb is to defragment whenever fragmentation exceeds 10%. For most drives, once every month or two is sufficient.

SOLUTION #2: Data on the drive has become fragmented. Back up the entire drive, reformat it, and restore the drive's contents from the backup. If you don't have a defragmentation utility or don't feel like springing for one, this is the easiest way to eliminate fragmentation. When files are restored from backup to your reformatted hard disk, they are copied in contiguous segments— eliminating the original fragmentation. Of course, as with the defragmentation utilities, the minute you start adding new files or modifying existing ones on the drive, fragmentation begins anew.

PROBLEM: Although it's working, I think there's something wrong with my hard disk (*vague feelings of dread*).

SOLUTION: Buy and use a general hard disk utility package, such as Norton Utilities for the Mac (Symantec), 911 Utilities (Microcom), or Central Point MacTools.

When you aren't sure what the problem is (as in "Gee, strange things are happening with my hard disk."), the best place to start is with a general hard disk utility package. Follow the instructions and run the program's diagnostic tools on each hard disk and partition. Then follow the utility's recommendations. If the problem is a simple one, the program may be able to both diagnose and correct it for you. These packages also provide ways for you to undelete files (recover files that you have erased), scan disks for bad sectors, and check individual files for damage.

As a general preventative measure, it's a good idea to run the hard disk diagnostics every couple of weeks. Many problems are easier to correct when they're caught early. In some cases, the utility will let you know about problems you didn't realize you had.

TIP

Until you buy one of the general hard disk utility packages, you can use the Disk First Aid program that comes with the system software. Although it isn't as thorough as the commercial packages, it can identify and correct several common hard disk problems. Always make sure the utility is compatible with the current version of the system software you're using! Old Norton Utilities for the Mac versions trashed System 7 disks when System 7 was first released.

CAUTION

Test software provided by a drive manufacturer may only work properly with their particular hard disks. Using any part of this software on other brands of hard disks can have serious consequences. (That's how I trashed my first hard disk....)

PROBLEM: I have a hard disk *testing* utility. Is it possible to damage my data by using this program?

SOLUTION: Dangerous hard disk tests are usually marked as destructive (they will overwrite existing data during the testing process). If the instructions do not clearly distinguish between destructive and nondestructive tests, do not use the testing program.

Hard Disk Startup Problems

PROBLEM: The Mac refuses to boot from my hard disk. Instead of booting, I see a disk icon with a question mark on it.

SOLUTION #1: There isn't a valid System Folder on the hard disk. Install one. In order to qualify as a boot drive, the disk must contain a valid System Folder at its root (main) level. To be valid, the folder must be "blessed" by the system. If the folder is indeed valid, the system software will automatically change the appearance of the folder to match that shown in Figure 3.4. If you don't have a blessed System Folder, you should reinstall your system software (see Chapter 2).

Figure 3.4

Valid System Folder icons.

SOLUTION #2: The drive has not been set as the Startup Disk. With any Mac after the Plus, you specify a startup disk in the Startup Device (System 6) or Startup Disk (System 7) control panel.

When you install the system software on a particular disk, it is automatically selected as the startup disk. Occasionally, however, the Mac can lose track of this information. To check your current startup disk or specify a new one under System 7, do the following:

1. Select the **Control Panels** desk accessory from the **Apple** menu. The folder containing your control panel documents will open.

2. Double-click the Startup Disk Control Panel icon to open that Control Panel (see Figure 3.5).

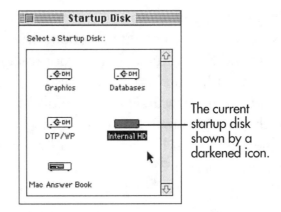

Figure 3.5

The Startup Disk control panel.

The current startup disk shown by a darkened icon.

3. The current startup disk (if there is one) is indicated by a darkened disk icon. To select a different one, click on the appropriate icon.

4. To save your changes, click the close box in the Startup Disk window.

If you are using System 6, a similar procedure is used with the Startup Device control panel.

TIP

If you have a Mac Plus, you do not use the control panel to specify the startup device. On a Plus, the device with the highest SCSI ID number is assumed to be the startup device. If you have multiple SCSI devices, be sure that the one with the System Folder is given the highest ID number (6 or less).

SOLUTION #3: If you have external SCSI devices (hard disks or a scanner, for instance), SCSI problems may be preventing your boot drive from mounting or being read correctly. See "Setting Up a Hard Disk (and Other SCSI Devices)" earlier in this chapter for help in identifying the cause of the problem.

SOLUTION #4: You have a hardware problem with the hard disk that requires a dealer's attention.

PROBLEM: My external hard disk didn't appear on the desktop when I booted the system.

SOLUTION #1: The drive may not have had time to warm up. Reboot the system using the Special menu's **Restart** command. All external hard disks must be on and warmed up *before* you turn on the Mac.

SOLUTION #2: Use a utility such as SCSI Tools (see Figure 3.6) to mount the disk (make it appear on the desktop). SCSI Tools, a shareware Control Panel device, can be used to mount reluctant drives. Clicking the Mount button causes the utility to scan the SCSI chain and display any legitimate drives that are not already on the desktop. There are many *CDEVs* (Control Panel devices) and desk accessories that offer this function.

Figure 3.6

The SCSI Tools CDEV.

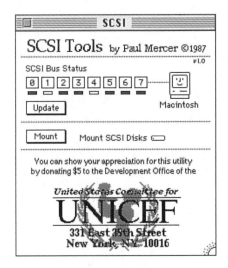

SOLUTION #3: If the disk is a removable hard disk or CD-ROM, it may need special driver software to make it appear on the desktop. Check the software that came with the drive and make sure that you have installed it correctly.

SOLUTION #4: If you've just installed a new version of the system software, the hard disk's driver software may not be compatible with it. If this is the case, you will probably have problems with the drive the first time you attempt to use it after installing the new system software. Contact the drive manufacturer to see about getting a new driver. Until the driver is sent to you, you will have to reinstall the old system software if you want to continue using the disk.

PROBLEM: Instead of showing me the desktop at startup, I see a Sad Mac icon (a Mac with a frowning face and x's for eyes).

SOLUTION #1: The Mac has encountered a serious hardware or software problem. One possible cause is that the startup disk's boot blocks have been damaged.

To check this, restart the Macintosh from a floppy disk, such as the system software's Disk Tools disk. If this doesn't work, it's likely that the problem has a different cause—one that's unrelated to your hard disk. See Chapter 2 for other causes of the sad Mac face.

On the other hand, if booting from the floppy does work, the hard disk's boot blocks may need to be repaired or replaced. There are two ways to do this:

- Use a hard disk utility to repair the boot blocks.

- Replace the System file on the hard disk by reinstalling the system software. (You can use the system software's Installer program to accomplish this. See Chapter 2 for the necessary steps.)

SOLUTION #2: SCSI problems occasionally cause this. See the section earlier in this chapter on setting up a hard drive.

Miscellaneous Hard Disk Problems

PROBLEM: I *formatted* (erased) my hard disk by mistake. Is there anything I can do to get my data back?

SOLUTION #1: Many of the hard disk maintenance packages discussed in this chapter include a routine that will enable you to recover from an accidental formatting. When a hard disk is formatted, the data itself is not erased. Instead, the system software merely marks all the disk space as available for new data. Thus, whatever you do, do *not* install the recovery program on the newly formatted hard disk. Doing so puts your old data at risk of being overwritten. As soon as you notice the error, run the recovery program from the original floppy or a copy of it, and follow the software's instructions for recovering the data. (Note: Formatting a floppy disk, on the other hand, really does delete the data and is not a situation from which you can recover.)

SOLUTION #2: Restore the hard disk from your most recent backup. (You probably thought of this one yourself.) Since every file that has been added or changed since the last backup will be lost, this should definitely be considered the approach of last resort.

▼ **TIP**

If you copied any files to the hard disk before running the recovery program in Solution #1, be sure to check your backup disks or tapes. You may be able to recover the destroyed files (those listed as unrecoverable by the utility program) by restoring them from the backup.

PROBLEM: I have a removable hard disk. How do I *dismount* it (get it off the desktop) so that I can insert a different cartridge?

SOLUTION: Drag it to the Trash. There are two situations in which you will want to dismount a removable hard disk: when shutting down the Mac, and when you want to insert a different cartridge. In either case, it is done in the same way that you eject a floppy: you drag its icon to the Trash can. Once the icon for the removable hard disk has disappeared from the desktop, you can safely use the drive's eject button to remove the cartridge.

PROBLEM: Why doesn't my tape drive show up on the desktop like my hard disk and floppies do?

SOLUTION: Most tape drives are not *mountable*. They will never show up on the desktop. Whether a SCSI device is mountable or not depends on the driver software that the manufacturer provides. The vast majority of tape drive manufacturers agree that it is best not to have the drive be treated as a desktop device—like a hard disk, for instance. Hard drives can randomly access any part of the disk. Tapes, on the other hand, are *sequential* devices. In order to get from one part of a tape to another, they must move through all the tape in between. Although making a tape drive mountable would allow you to launch programs from it, for example, you probably wouldn't be delighted with the amount of time it would take.

Floppy Disk Issues

Disks that can be used in your Mac's floppy drive can have any of three capacities, depending on the particular drive you have: 400K, 800K, or 1.4M.

Macs prior to the Mac Plus (the 128K and 512K) all had floppy drives that were designed to use only single-sided, double-density floppies (400K). Starting with the Mac Plus, the floppy drive could handle 400K or 800K (double-sided, double-density) floppies.

Newer Macs all contain Apple's SuperDrive, and can read and write 400K, 800K, or 1.4M floppies. Currently, only the 800K and 1.4M floppies are in common use.

TIP

There isn't any difference between blank PC and Mac floppies. Basically, 3.5" disks are all the same. They only become Mac or PC floppies after you format *them (use the system software to make them ready to receive data). You should note that some floppies are sold already formatted. Although you can reformat disks that have been preformatted for the IBM PC, it's silly to pay extra for them.*

Although all 3.5" floppies look basically alike, the 1.4M disks usually have two distinguishing characteristics: they are stamped with an "HD" emblem and have a permanent hole punched in the upper-left corner (opposite from the write-enable/write-protect hole in the upper right corner—see Figure 3.7).

When a floppy is inserted, the SuperDrive's sensors look for the extra hole. If it is found, the drive treats the disk as a high-density floppy. If the hole isn't there, the drive assumes that it is looking at a 400K or 800K floppy. After determining the disk type of a blank floppy, the

Mac uses this information to present you with the appropriate formatting options. This prevents you from accidentally formatting a high-density disk as a low-density one and vice versa.

800K
Floppy

1.4M
Floppy

Figure 3.7

Floppy disks: 800K versus 1.4M. (Illustration courtesy of EPS Business Art by T/Maker Company.)

Then how can you tell a 400K floppy from an 800K one? These two kinds of disks have no distinguishing physical characteristics that set them apart. If the manufacturer has seen fit to do so, however, they might be marked as follows (usually on the metal shutter or on the back of the disk):

- 400K: Single Sided or MF1-DD
- 800K: Double Sided or MF2-DD
- 1.4M: MF2-HD

Floppy Disk Problems

PROBLEM: The Mac is telling me `This disk is unreadable` (see Figure 3.8).

SOLUTION #1: You have inserted an *unformatted* (blank) floppy into the drive. It must be formatted before it can be used by the Mac. If you are certain that the disk does not contain data, click the button marked **Two-Sided** to format the disk. After it has been formatted, it will be usable for storing data and program files.

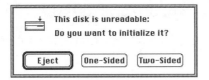

> ## CAUTION
>
> *It is possible to format a single-sided, double-density disk as an 800K disk just by selecting the double-sided formatting option. You can also buy a special disk punch to fool the Mac into thinking that an 800K disk is actually a 1.4M floppy. Doing so, however, is a bad idea. Although the floppy may initially hold data and appear to be working properly, it is not certified for storing that amount of information—it's a disaster waiting to happen.*

Figure 3.8

The "unreadable disk" alert.

NOTE

*If you insert a blank high-density floppy into the drive, the choices in the dialog box will be different. The options are to **Eject** or to **Initialize** it. The Mac instantly recognizes a high-density disk by the permanent hole it has in the upper left-hand corner. All high-density disks will automatically be formatted for the proper capacity: 1.4M.*

SOLUTION #2: You have inserted a high-density floppy into a low-density drive. Only Macs equipped with the Apple SuperDrive can read high-density (1.4M) floppies. To use the data on this disk, you should eject it, insert it into a Mac that is equipped with a SuperDrive, and copy its data to one or more 800K floppies.

SOLUTION #3: This message can also be displayed for a disk that contains valid Macintosh data, but has become damaged. If you believe (or know) that there's data on the disk, do not initialize it! Initializing a floppy permanently deletes any data that may be on the disk. Instead, you should follow the steps listed in the next chapter for recovering files from damaged disks.

PROBLEM: The Mac is telling me `This is not a Macintosh disk` (see Figure 3.9).

SOLUTION: The disk has been previously formatted for use on another type of computer, such as a PC or an Amiga.

> **CAUTION**
>
> *The disk may contain valid data meant for another computer system. Click the Eject button or you will destroy the contents of the disk!*

If you don't care about what's on the disk and simply want to reformat it for use on a Mac, click the **Two-Sided** button. If, on the other hand, you meant to move the data to the Mac, do the following:

1. Click the **Eject** button to eject the floppy from the drive.

2. Run the Apple File Exchange program that came with your system software.

3. Once the program is running, you can insert the foreign floppy and interpret its contents. (See the manuals that came with your Mac for instructions on using Apple File Exchange.)

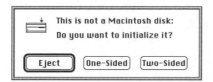

Figure 3.9

The "not a Macintosh disk" alert.

PROBLEM: The Mac is telling me that the floppy I've just inserted "needs minor repairs."

SOLUTION: This message just means that there's a small problem with the disk's directory. Click the OK button to repair the disk.

PROBLEM: I just tried to format a floppy and the Mac is telling me that the "format verification failed."

SOLUTION: The floppy cannot reliably hold data. Try formatting the disk again. If it still fails, throw the disk away.

PROBLEM: I'm copying some files from one disk to another, and the Mac is telling me that a file `couldn't be verified, because a disk error occurred` (see Figure 3.10).

SOLUTION: Either the disk you are attempting to copy to or the spot on the original disk where the file is stored contains *bad sectors*; in other words, that part of the media can no longer store data. (Note: This message can occur regardless of the type of disk you are using: floppy, hard disk, removable cartridge, and so on.)

Figure 3.10

Disk errors during copying.

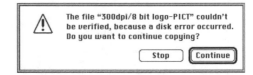

Begin by clicking the **Continue** button. This forces the Finder to reattempt the copy. Occasionally, the copy will finish correctly.

If that doesn't work, try copying the files to a different disk. If you're successful, it means that there was nothing wrong with the files. The disk you originally attempted to copy the files to, however, contains bad sectors. If it's a fixed or removable hard disk, you should use any of the popular hard disk utility packages (or the one that came with the drive) to scan the disk for bad sectors and mark them as unusable. This will prevent future problems with that portion of the disk. Reformatting the disk will also mark the bad sectors for you.

TIP

Although you can use this same procedure to mark bad spots on floppies, too, it may be false economy. If you compare the value of your data to the cost of a floppy, it's cheaper to throw out suspect floppies.

If copying the files to a different disk still results in this error message, it means that the file is damaged. See the next chapter for help with recovering data from a damaged file.

PROBLEM: The Mac is asking me to swap a pair of floppies over and over again.

SOLUTION #1: Continue swapping disks as requested. Believe it or not, you will eventually finish.

This problem happens most often when:

- your startup disk (the one with the System Folder that you used to boot the Mac) is a floppy,

  or

- you have a single floppy drive and are attempting to copy files from one floppy to another.

Information from the System Folder is critical to many programs. If you eject your startup floppy so you can launch a program from a different disk whenever the program or system software needs to use system resources (to draw a window or display a font, for example), it will interrupt your work and ask you to reinsert the startup floppy so it can load the needed resources. Then, when another piece of the program is needed, it will ask you to insert the program disk (and on and on).

SOLUTION #2: This can sometimes be caused by leaving "ghosts" of disks on the desktop (by using the **Eject** command instead of dragging the disks to the Trash). If a disk is no longer needed on the desktop, drag it to the Trash.

SOLUTION #3: Press ⌘-. (period) to halt the procedure. This is useful when you want to abort a disk-to-disk copy. You can also issue this command while running a program. Note, however, that although the program should provide a graceful way of handling this command, it may not.

PROBLEM: The copy I just made of this program disk doesn't work.

SOLUTION: If the disk is copy-protected or only runs from an exact duplicate, a Finder-made copy of the disk will not work. When you hear or read that a program is *copy-protected* it sometimes means that the publisher has done something to the program disk to prevent you from copying it. (There are other more innocuous forms of copy-protection, such as requiring the individual to personalize the software by entering his or her name and a serial number the first time that the software is used, for example.)

Another reason that copies of some program disks don't work is because sometimes they must be *exact* copies. Only an *image* copy (an exact sector-for-sector duplicate) of the System 7 software disks, for example, will work. Such disks must be copied with an image- or sector-copy program rather than with the Finder. (The Finder only makes file-by-file copies; the precise *locations* that the files are copied to on the target disk are treated as irrelevant.) Two programs that are capable of performing an image copy include Floppier (part of Symantec's Norton Utilities package) and Disk Copy (Apple Computer).

PROBLEM: I don't have a hard disk, so I run all my programs from floppies. How can I save data files to a floppy other than the program disk?

SOLUTION: When you issue a **Save** or **Save As...** command, you can select the disk on which you want to save the current file. Click the **Drive** (System 6) or **Desktop** button (System 7) to select the floppy disk that's currently in the drive. Then click the **Eject** button. After the floppy has popped out, you can insert a different disk, select it, and save your file. If the program later needs information from its own disk again, it will eject your data disk and tell you to insert the program disk.

Many older Macs came with only a floppy drive. Under older versions of the system software (System 6 and earlier), it was feasible to run many Mac programs from this single drive. The down side, however, was that the Mac was constantly asking you to swap disks (switching between the startup, the program, and data disks). System 7, however, makes single-floppy operation almost impossible. Even installing a minimal version of System 7 on a high-density floppy leaves little room for programs. A minimal copy of System 7 for a IIci, for example, has only 300K left over—even less if you also install the printer software. The interminable System 6 disk swapping and the increased size of System 7 are both excellent reasons for buying a hard disk.

PROBLEM: A floppy disk is jammed in my drive. How can I get it out?

SOLUTION #1: Issue the Mac's **Eject** command: ⌘-**Shift-1** to eject a disk in an internal floppy drive or ⌘-**Shift-2** to eject a disk in an external floppy drive.

SOLUTION #2: Quit all programs and select the **Restart** command from the **Special** menu (see Figure 3.11). When restarting, hold down the button on your mouse or trackball. This is the startup command to eject all floppies.

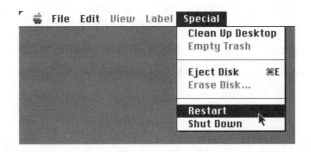

Figure 3.11

Selecting the Restart command.

SOLUTION #3: Insert the end of a large straightened paper clip into the tiny hole next to the floppy drive slot and push it straight in. In most cases, this will forcibly eject the floppy.

SOLUTION #4: Take the Mac to a dealer for repair.

If disks frequently get stuck in the drive, it's probably time for a visit to the repair shop. On the other hand, if only one particular floppy continually gets stuck, you should copy its data to another disk and then throw away the bad floppy.

Floppy Safety Precautions

Although the 3.5" floppies used with the Mac are protected by a hard plastic case that makes them seem indestructible, it is possible to damage the disks and the data they contain. Here are a few simple precautions you can take to avoid the Dead Disk Blues:

Rule #1: No Magnets, Please!

Disks and tapes of all types are *magnetic media*. The information contained on them is stored there magnetically. Contact with a magnet is the fastest way to scramble a disk or tape. (That's what a bulk eraser is, by the way—a giant magnet used to quickly erase tapes.) Keep in mind that magnets take many forms—including magnetized paper clip dispensers and the insides of most electronic devices (telephones, monitors, and printers, for example). Be careful where you stack your floppies.

Rule #2: Hands Off the Inner Surface of the Disk

The metal shutter protects the disk inside its case. It automatically slides back when you pop the floppy into your Mac and then closes when you eject it. You can slide it back to take a peek at the disk if you like, but don't touch the disk material. The oil from your fingerprint can easily destroy your data.

Rule #3: Avoid Extremes in Temperature

Floppies can tolerate a wide range of temperatures, but it's not smart to leave them in your car when it's 100 degrees outside or toss them in a northern Minnesota snow bank (although I can't imagine why you might try the latter). When I moved from the northeast to the desert, my computer and floppies sat in a moving van for almost two weeks in 120 degree temperatures. I lost *dozens* of floppies.

Rule #4: Watch Out for Static Electricity

Static electricity can do just as much damage to a floppy as a magnet. If you have seasonal static problems, you may want to check out some of the antistatic options discussed in Chapter 1.

Rule #5: Lock your Program Disks

Every floppy drive has a sensor that checks the hole in the upper right corner of the floppy. If the hole is open, the disk is considered *locked* (data can be read from it, but no modifications can be made to the contents of the disk). If the hole is closed, the disk is *write-enabled* (data can be read from the disk *and* modified). In general, you should lock any disk that holds files that you want to keep from changing. A good example is a master disk that contains any new program you've purchased. Unless stated otherwise in a program's installation instructions, you should lock every program disk before installing its contents to your hard disk, running programs on that disk, or copying it to a different floppy.

Immediately locking a program floppy will also prevent it from being infected by a virus. If the disk can't be written to, it can't be infected.

Moving On

Disk problems are particularly scary because they often concern the safety of your data. With common sense and the proper utility programs, though, you should be able to resolve most disk problems without having to place a frantic call to your dealer. In the next chapter, we'll deal with a closely related issue—problems with files.

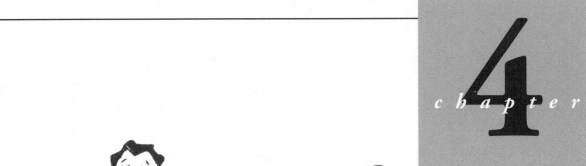

Problems with Files

Open any disk window and you'll find files: documents, programs, desk accessories, fonts, system files, and more. Much of your Macintosh work involves manipulating files—opening and saving them, copying them to other disks, and throwing them in the Trash. This chapter discusses many of the most common file problems, and also presents solutions for handling deleted, damaged, and misplaced files.

File- and Folder-Naming Conventions

If you owned a PC before getting your Mac, you'll be surprised and delighted at the freedom the Mac offers in naming files and folders. PC file names are restricted to eight characters, making most file names end up looking like nonsense syllables. Mac file and folder names, on the other hand, can be up to 31 characters long! Giving clear, easily-understood names to your files and folders is a good way to start getting organized.

PROBLEM: I'm trying to save a file from within a program and keep getting an error message saying that the file name is illegal or contains a bad character.

SOLUTION: Other than the 31-character limit, the only restriction on file and folder names is that they may not contain the colon (:) character. If you try to enter a colon when naming a file or folder on the desktop, the system software will automatically protect you by substituting a hyphen (-) for each colon. Attempting to enter a colon when saving a file from within a program will usually result in the keystroke being ignored (nothing happens when you press it), or an error message will appear. If the latter happens, you can fix things by typing a file name without any colons.

PROBLEM: I've typed a name for a folder, and the Mac is telling me that the name is already taken.

SOLUTION: There is another file or folder on the same level as the newly named folder that is already using that name. Name the new folder something different.

Oops! I Threw It in the Trash

Sooner or later it happens to everyone. The annual report that you've slaved over for days is accidentally tossed into the Trash or becomes mysteriously unreadable. No matter how careful you are, this *will* happen to you. Preventative measures, however, are simple. Follow them carefully, and you can minimize the damage and increase the likelihood of a successful recovery.

If you haven't emptied the Trash (by selecting Empty Trash in the Finder's Special menu), your file hasn't been deleted. It's still sitting in the Trash. To retrieve a file from the Trash:

1. *Return to the Finder Desktop and double-click the **Trash** icon.*

2. *Drag the desired files or folders out of the Trash and move them back to the icon of any mounted disk.*

Save Immediately and Save Often

When you create a new document in a program, it is often given a temporary name such as "Untitled 1." After doing a little work on the document, you should save it to disk using the program's **Save** or **Save As...** command. Until you save, any work that you've done on the document is only in your computer's memory. If you were to turn off the computer without saving—or if a power failure abruptly turned off the Mac *for* you—the entire document would be lost forever.

After the document has been saved, you should be sure to use the Save command frequently. Regardless of how much you've typed, the file on disk (the permanent record of your work) is only as current as your last Save. Quit the program without saving and any changes you have made to the document will disappear into the ether.

How often should you save? The easiest way to figure this out is to ask yourself a different question: "How much work can I afford to lose?" As a writer, reconstructing more than a paragraph of a word processing document is painful to me. So, at a minimum, I issue a Save command every time I start a new paragraph or make a significant change to a document.

If you're the type of person who often forgets to save regularly, take a glance through your program's manual. Many programs now include an *autosave* option that automatically saves your work at designated time intervals (every 5 minutes, for example) or after a certain number of keystrokes. Some programs also have an *automatic backup* option that instructs the program to keep intact the original copy of every file when you open one for editing. If your programs don't include these features, you may want to explore some of the commercial utility programs that enable you to add autosave to any or all of your favorite programs. AutoSave II from Magic Software is one such utility.

Some programs, such as PageMaker and Microsoft Word, can do "mini-saves" (or fast saves as they are sometimes called), which record minor changes in documents for you. If you forget to save a document or the Mac crashes before you get an opportunity to save, there's a chance that your work will be stored as a mini-save in a temporary file. See your program's manual to see if this feature is provided and for instructions on resurrecting data from a mini-saved file.

A few programs, such as HyperCard and FileMaker Pro, take file saving out of your hands. As a protection against losing data, these programs automatically save your work for you. The advantage is that you never have to remember to save—it's done for you. The disadvantage is that all of your changes—including the bad ones—are automatically saved. Getting back to your original version can be a lot of work. As a protection against inadvertent saves, you may want to make a backup copy of your file before starting the program. The simplest way to do this is to:

1. Go to the desktop and click once on the data file icon to select it.

2. Select **Duplicate** (⌘-**D**) from the **File** menu. Your Mac displays the dialog box shown in Figure 4.1 as it duplicates the file.

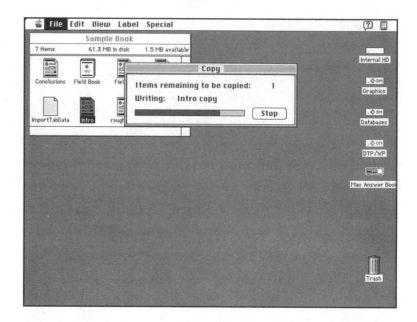

Figure 4.1

Duplicating a file (System 7).

Suppose the file is named Intro. If you are running System 7, the duplicate will be named Intro copy. Under System 6, it would be called Copy of Intro. You can open either the original or the copy, and use the other file as a backup. If you're happy with the new changes made to the file, you can throw away the duplicate at the end of the computing session.

Keep Multiple Copies

Just as most people keep multiple copies of important documents, such as tax returns, it's a good idea to keep multiple copies of your most important data files. The simplest way to protect data is to make a second copy of it. Most data documents will fit on an 800K or 1.4M floppy. To copy a file from a hard disk to a floppy, just click on the file's icon and drag it to the floppy's icon. For added safety, you may want to store the floppy at a location different from your Mac to protect it from a fire, flood, or a tornado that could destroy your office.

Depending on your computing practices, you may also want to keep several generations of certain files. Business reports, worksheets, and computer programs, for instance, may go through several drafts before they're completed. If you just use the Save command over and over, all previous versions of the document are overwritten each time you save. Remember that bright idea you cut out of the document three revisions ago? It's gone. One way around this is to use the Save As... command rather than Save. Save As... enables you to save a document with a new name. If you use a new name along with a numbering scheme (Report 1, Report 2, and so on), each Save As... will result in another disk file that you can later go back to or cut-and-paste from as necessary.

Some files (large databases, desktop publishing files, and complex graphics, for instance) may *not* fit on a single floppy. Archiving compression programs such as Compact Pro, StuffIt Deluxe, and DiskDoubler can split large files across several floppies. The same program can later be used to reconstruct the pieces of the split file and restore it to your hard disk.

Finally, if you have a hard disk, you should seriously consider a *backup* program—a more formal approach to creating an extra copy of important data. Backup programs can copy the entire contents of your hard disk (or selected folders and files) to a series of floppies, a removable hard disk, or tape. Some of the best commercial backup programs include Retrospect and Fastback II (for backing up and archiving to almost any media, including tapes) and DiskFit Pro and Redux (for floppy backups).

Install an "Undelete" Utility

After a file has been tossed into the Trash and the Trash has been emptied, the common conception is that the file has been irretrievably erased. Guess again! The Mac doesn't actually erase anything. Instead, it takes the space where the file is located and merely marks it as available for new files. The next time you create a file or change an existing one, the system checks for unassigned disk space and, if necessary, may overwrite all or part of your previously deleted file.

In order to successfully retrieve a deleted file, you'll need to buy a special *undelete* utility. My personal favorite is Complete Undelete, a Control Panel device that comes as a part of 911 Utilities (Microcom). Norton Utilities, Central Point MacTools, and many other troubleshooting packages also include their own undelete utilities.

Here's an example of how you would undelete a file. To use Complete Undelete to retrieve one or more deleted files, you do the following. (This assumes that you have previously used Complete Undelete to install a delete tracking log for the disk in question. If not, Complete Undelete will not be able to retrieve your deleted files.)

1. Open the Complete Undelete CDEV (see Figure 4.2).

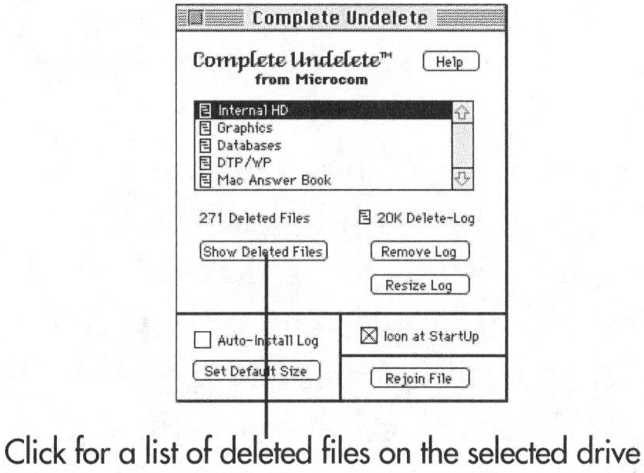

Click for a list of deleted files on the selected drive

Figure 4.2

The Undelete CDEV displays a list of all drives connected to your Mac. Ones that have a delete tracking log installed are indicated by a small text page icon.

2. Click on the name of the drive from which you are attempting to recover deleted files.

3. Click the **Show Deleted Files** button. A list of files like the one in Figure 4.3 is presented. You can now select files to undelete.

Figure 4.3

The Deleted Files list shows the status of each deleted file on the disk.

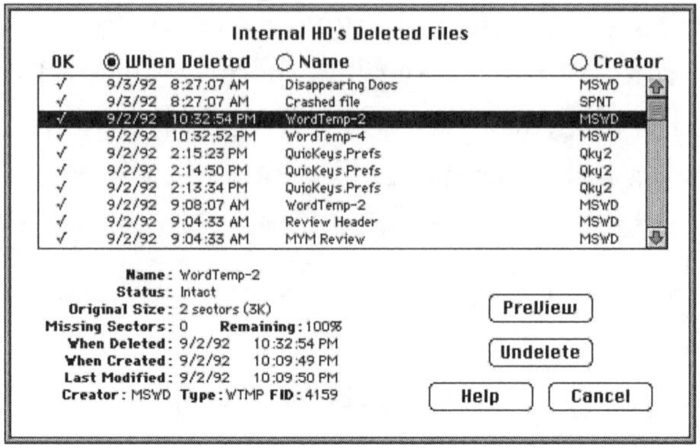

CAUTION

Before attempting to retrieve a deleted file, there is one cardinal rule to remember. No matter which utility you're using, don't do anything to the data disk that would cause information to be written onto it. This includes initializing or erasing the disk, copying software to it, or saving any files. As long as nothing new has been written to the disk, there's an excellent chance that your previous file or files are still intact.

A file that is preceded by a check mark is still intact and can be successfully recovered. Files that are not shown with a check mark may still be partially intact. When attempting to restore a partially over-written file, you can instruct Complete Undelete to extract only the text portion of the file and, option-ally, to fill any holes in the file with a string of zeros. This increases the likelihood that the file can still be opened by the program in which it was created.

If your undelete utility is already on your hard disk, run it and follow its instructions for recovering deleted files. If you haven't installed the utility, follow its instructions for exhuming deleted files by running the utility from its original disk. As an added precaution, you should save any recovered files on a disk other than the one from which they were recovered—assuming that the undelete utility allows you to specify a destination disk.

> **TIP**
>
> *Other utilities (discussed below) can also help you recover from an accidentally formatted (erased) hard disk. Erasing a floppy disk, on the other hand, is not a situation from which you can recover. Erasing a floppy really erases it.*

"Munged" Files

Although it happens infrequently, sometimes a file becomes damaged, rendering its contents unreadable. (Of course, you won't know that this has happened until you try to open the file later.) If your Mac crashes while the file is being saved, for instance, there is a high probability that the file in question may now be unusable. Knowing that this occasionally happens, some programs provide a recovery procedure. Others may create a temporary file (often stored in the System Folder) as a backup in case of a crash.

If you are running System 7, there's one more place to look. Check the contents of the Trash can. There may be a folder called "Rescued items from *disk name*" (see Figure 4.4). If you're lucky, when you open the folder, you may find a readable copy of the file you were working on when the Mac went boom.

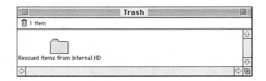

Figure 4.4

Following a crash under System 7, be sure to check the Trash for folders like this one.

Guess what? While writing this very chapter, my Mac crashed before I had a chance to Save. In the Trash was a Microsoft Word file called "WordTemp-1"—shown in Figure 4.5—that enabled me to recover a large portion of the work.

Let's say, on the other hand, that you weren't so lucky. None of the previous suggestions helped or were applicable. What else can you do? If the file contained text or pictures, CanOpener 2 from Abbott Systems (see Figure 4.6) may be able to help. Damaged or not, CanOpener 2 lets you examine the text and picture portions of any file. Once the file is opened in CanOpener, you can copy all the usable text and pictures and then paste them into a new document.

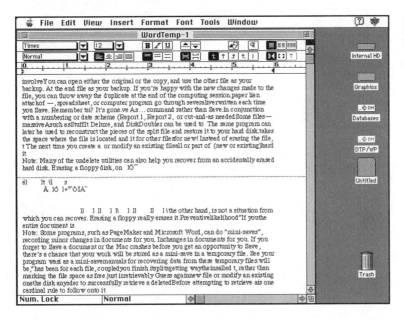

Figure 4.5

Although a far cry from the original text, the recovered text shows all edit changes that were made to the chapter. Twenty minutes of cutting and pasting sure beats trying to reconstruct the changes from memory.

The Case of the Disappearing Document

PROBLEM: I can't remember where I stored one of my files.

SOLUTION: Unless your hard disk is very organized or you have an exceptional memory, it's easy to forget where you placed a particular data file or program. Rather than opening each folder and subfolder to find the file, you can use the system software to help you search.

Figure 4.6

Since CanOpener can open almost any file, you may want to do a little exploration. Here's an interesting text segment that I discovered in the System file.

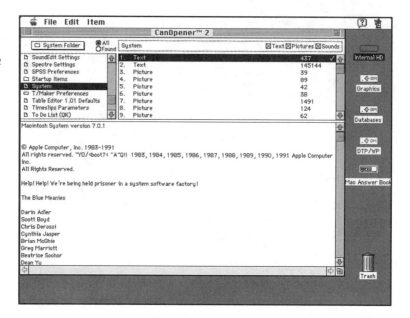

The Find File desk accessory in System 6 allows you to search one or more attached drives for a particular file according to its name. In System 7, the Find command (located in the File menu) allows you to search for a file by name, size, kind, label, creation date, modification date, version, comments, or lock status.

If you frequently lose files or have extremely large hard disk volumes that you must search, you may be happier with one of the commercial file finder utilities. Several popular file finders, such as GOfer (Microlytics) can open and examine the text in files during a search.

DiskTop Find's (CE Software) search commands are similar to those provided by System 7's Find, but you can also use it to search for files by the program they were created in (finding only Microsoft Excel files, for instance) and to combine multiple search criteria.

Copying Files

PROBLEM: How do you copy a file from one floppy to another when you only have one floppy drive?

SOLUTION: Follow these steps:

1. Go to the Finder Desktop.

2. Insert the disk that you wish to copy *from* into your disk drive. (In this example, the source floppy is named Source Disk.)

3. Open the disk's window by double-clicking on the floppy icon so you can see the file or files that you wish to copy.

4. Issue the Finder's **Eject Disk** command by pressing ⌘-**E** or by selecting **Eject Disk** from the **Special** menu. This leaves a grayed-out image of the disk and its files on the desktop (see Figure 4.7).

5. Insert the destination disk into the floppy drive. (In this example, the destination floppy is named Target Disk.)

6. Select the grayed-out files or folders on the source disk that you wish to copy, and drag their images to the target disk's icon. The Mac instructs you to swap disks as it needs them.

When the copy is finished, you can drag the disk icons to the Trash if you want to remove them from the desktop.

Figure 4.7

Using the Eject Disk command on a floppy leaves a "ghost" or grayed-out image of the disk, its windows, and files on the desktop.

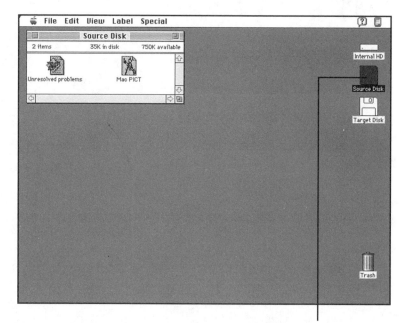

The grayed-out disk image

PROBLEM: When I try to copy a file to another location on the disk that it's already on, it only gets moved—not copied.

SOLUTION #1: Use the Finder's **Duplicate** command (choose **Duplicate** from the **File** menu) to create a second copy of the file, move the copy to the new location, and then change its name. If the file is being copied to a different folder on the disk, you can even rename it using its original file name.

SOLUTION #2: Use a utility program, such as DiskTop (from CE Software), to copy the file. As long as you are copying the file to a different level of the disk (into a folder, for example), the copy will even retain the original file name.

SOLUTION #3: If you're running System 7, you may prefer to make an *alias* of the file rather than a complete copy. An alias is merely a pointer to a particular file, folder, or disk. Double-clicking an alias instructs the system software to open the real copy of the file, folder, or disk. To create an alias, click once to select the file, folder, or disk, and select **Make Alias** from the Finder's **File** menu.

PROBLEM: During a file copy, the Mac is telling me that a file "couldn't be written and was skipped (unknown error)."

SOLUTION: The file is probably damaged. Try copying the file to a different disk to make sure that this isn't a problem with the destination disk. If the Finder still can't make the copy without displaying this error message, the file is damaged. Use one of the file recovery programs discussed above or restore a copy of the file from your most recent backup.

PROBLEM: The Mac says that it can't copy or open a particular file.

SOLUTION: The area(s) of the disk in which the file is stored may contain bad sectors. When you first format a disk of any kind, the Mac's operating system checks it for *bad sectors* (sections of the disk that cannot reliably store data). If any are found, the operating system makes a note of them so that no files will be saved to those locations on the disk. Unfortunately, as you continue to use a disk, additional areas may go bad—ones that the system didn't originally identify and mark. In the best case, the bad sectors may not overlap with any of your files. In the worst case, the bad sector may be in the middle of an important data file. (On one particularly bad day, I lost an 800K PageMaker layout this way.)

Most programs will be unable to read a file that contains bad sectors and will report that the file is damaged. If you don't have a recent backup of the file, you may be able to open the damaged one with CanOpener 2 or one of the other hard disk utilities, and either repair the sectors or extract the usable portion of the file's contents.

TIP

To keep those bad sectors from destroying any additional files, you should immediately do a full backup of the drive, reformat it, and restore its contents from the backup. Reformatting the drive will mark the new bad sectors as unusable.

PROBLEM: The Mac is telling me that there isn't enough memory to copy a group of files.

SOLUTION #1: If you're using System 6, you can try increasing the Finder's memory allocation. Under System 6, the Finder is treated like a program. You can increase the amount of memory allocated to the Finder by doing the following:

1. Open the **System Folder** and click once on the **Finder** icon to select it.

2. Select **Get Info** from the Finder's **File** menu (or press ⌘-**I**).

3. Increase the Finder's memory allocation (Application Memory Size) by entering a new figure. If you can spare the memory, enter **320**.

4. Close the Info window, and retry the copy procedure.

The Finder's new memory allocation will also improve the speed with which Finder windows open and close. *(Note: Under System 7, you cannot change the Finder's memory allocation.)*

SOLUTION #2: Copy the files in two or more batches.

PROBLEM: The Mac is telling me that there isn't enough room on the destination disk to copy the currently selected files.

SOLUTION #1: Delete some files from the destination disk and try again.

SOLUTION #2: Copy the files to *multiple* disks.

SOLUTION #3: Use a file compression utility (DiskDoubler, StuffIt Deluxe, or Compact Pro, for example) to compress the files so they take up less space. Then copy them to the destination disk.

PROBLEM: I'm trying to copy a file to another location, and the Mac is asking me if I want to `Replace items with the same names with the selected items?` (System 6). Under System 7, the equivalent message reads: `An older` *(or newer)* `item named` *file name* `already exists in this location. Do you want to replace it with the one you're moving?`

SOLUTION: There is already a file with that name on the destination disk. Click **OK** only if you intended to replace that file with the one you're attempting to copy or move. Otherwise, click **Cancel**.

Miscellaneous File Problems

PROBLEM: When I double-click a document on the desktop, the Mac tells me that the ...Application is busy or missing or ...the application program that created it could not be found.

SOLUTION #1: You don't have a copy of the program that was used to create this document. Launch a program that you think *should* be able to load the document, and then attempt to read it using the program's Open or Import command. If it is a word processing document or graphics file, for instance, try opening the file with your particular word processing or graphics program.

SOLUTION #2: Some files *can't* be opened because they are not typical document files. Clicking a Control Panel or Start-up document under System 6 will produce this same message.

SOLUTION #3: You may actually have the necessary program, but the Mac can't locate it. Rebuild the desktop, as described in Chapter 2, and try again.

SOLUTION #4: Launch the program first and then attempt to load the document. As long as you have the creating program, this approach *always* works—unless the file has been damaged.

PROBLEM: I'm trying to throw away a file or folder, and the Mac is telling me that one or more of the files are "locked or in use."

SOLUTION #1: A file that is *in use* is one that is currently open in a program or in use by the system software. Quit the current program and try again. If this doesn't work, restarting the Mac will usually eliminate the problem.

SOLUTION #2: Locked files have a check mark in the Locked check box in their Info window. Return the file to the desktop, select **Get Info** from the **File** menu or press ⌘-**I**, and then click in the **Locked** check box to unlock the file. You should now be able to throw the file away.

SOLUTION #3: Hold down the **Option** key when selecting the **Empty Trash** command in the System 7 **Special** menu. Doing this instructs the system software to throw away all files that are in the Trash—regardless of the status of the Locked check box. If you are using System 6, hold down the **Option** key while dragging the file to the Trash to achieve the same effect.

NOTE

You cannot throw away active pieces of the system software, such as the Finder or System. Attempting to do so should produce a similar alert message. Also under System 7, it's possible to lock a file with the Sharing dialog box (in the File menu of Finder). Make sure that the `This file cannot be moved, renamed or deleted` *check box is cleared.*

PROBLEM: When I double-click a file that's in the Trash, the Mac tells me to `Please drag the item (or its application) out of the Trash` (System 6).

SOLUTION: You can't launch a program or document that's in the Trash. Drag it to a disk and *then* double-click the file to launch it. (Note: The System 7 error message for this situation is much clearer.)

PROBLEM: I've opened a locked file by double-clicking it or loading it from within a program, and the Mac is telling me that I won't be able to save any changes.

SOLUTION #1: If the file is locked, you will not be able to save it under its current name. If you need to save the file, use the program's **Save As...** command to save it under a *new* name, or save it to a different folder or disk.

SOLUTION #2: If the disk is locked, use **Save as...** to put it on a different volume.

PROBLEM: My files have lost their nifty icons!

SOLUTION #1: The Finder has lost the information necessary to link an icon with the file, so it is displaying it as a plain document. To relink the file with its icon, rebuild the desktop by holding down ⌘-**Option** while restarting the Mac.

SOLUTION #2: If rebuilding the desktop doesn't work, opening the document from its creating application and resaving it may be more effective. To reestablish the link, it is also sometimes necessary to copy the creating program into the folder where the files are stored, and then open the files.

PROBLEM: A friend has given me a file for which I don't have the creating program. Is there any way for me to view its contents?

SOLUTION #1: You may have a *different* program that is capable of opening the file. Under System 7, you can use *drag-and-drop* to see if you have a compatible program. To use drag-and-drop, you simply select the file and drag its icon onto any program icon. If the program can open the file, the program's icon will turn dark. Releasing the mouse button will automatically cause the program to launch and open the file.

On the other hand, there is no drag-and-drop under System 6. However, many programs are capable of interpreting files created elsewhere. It's not unusual for a word processing program to read a variety of document formats, for example. Check your program's Open and Import commands for supported file formats.

SOLUTION #2: Some utility programs, such as CanOpener 2 from Abbott Systems Inc., can peek into the contents of any file and show you the text and graphics inside.

Moving On

Several of the more common file-related problems are best tackled with a good set of utility programs. See Appendix B, "Troubleshooting Tools," for additional information about the programs discussed in this chapter. In the following chapter, we'll discuss printing, fonts, and related problems.

Printing and Font Problems

Before we get into a general discussion of printing and printer problems, it's important for you to have a basic understanding of the different types of printers and font technologies in use.

There are three basic classes of Macintosh printers: dot-matrix (the most popular are the various models of ImageWriter), ink-jet (the HP Deskwriter and Apple StyleWriter, for example), and laser printers (such as the Apple LaserWriters).

Dot-matrix printers use the Mac's *QuickDraw* ROM routines to form characters from the bitmapped screen fonts installed in the System file. Graphics, too, are QuickDraw renditions of the images that you see on-screen. Because they are based on screen resolutions, dot-matrix printouts are the lowest quality found among the three printer types.

Ink-jet printers are capable of producing the same dot-density print-outs as standard laser printers—300 dots per inch (dpi). However, ink-jet printers are extremely slow when compared to lasers. As such, the ink-jets are sort of a happy medium between dot-matrix and laser printers.

Currently, there are three classes of Mac-compatible laser printers: QuickDraw, PostScript, and TrueType. All three types are capable of printing at a resolution of 300 dpi, and some more expensive ones support even higher resolutions.

Like dot-matrix printers, the QuickDraw-based lasers rely on bitmapped screen fonts and the printer's built-in fonts, rather than using PostScript outline files (discussed later in this chapter). Such printers often include several built-in fonts that, when used in a document, produce superior quality output. The quality of printed graphics, however, is limited to that of QuickDraw (72 dpi).

PostScript-equipped lasers are the current standard for high-end Macintosh printers. In addition to a set of built-in PostScript printer fonts, these printers can create exceptional quality text output from PostScript outline files. During a print job, the system software searches the printer and the System Folder for the necessary PostScript outline files. These files contain mathematical descriptions of every character in the font. Because the descriptions are mathematical, the characters can be smoothly scaled to any size.

> *PostScript is a programming language that is used to describe how to "draw" letters and graphics. PostScript printers contain a PostScript interpreter in the printer's ROM that can make sense of the commands that are being received from the PostScript printer driver in the Mac. High-definition graphics from programs such as Adobe Illustrator and Aldus Freehand are sent to the printer as detailed PostScript files rather than as screen images, which results in excellent quality output.*

TrueType is a font definition recently championed by Apple Computer and is a standard component of System 7. Unlike PostScript, the same TrueType fonts are used to create both printed and on-screen characters. (PostScript fonts are generally created from a *pair* of font files: an outline font for printing and a bitmapped font for screen display.) There are relatively few TrueType-based laser printers. Examples include the Apple LaserWriter IIf and the IIg. TrueType is *device-independent*; it can be used with *any* printer.

Using the Chooser

The Chooser desk accessory (Figure 5.1) enables you to select different printers for different print jobs, specify the port to which your printer cable is connected, and set special options (such as background print-ing) for each printer.

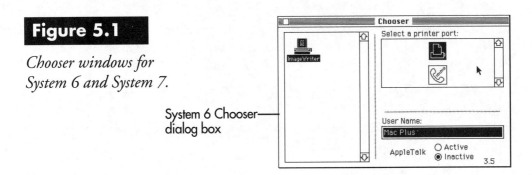

Figure 5.1

*Chooser windows for
System 6 and System 7.*

System 6 Chooser
dialog box

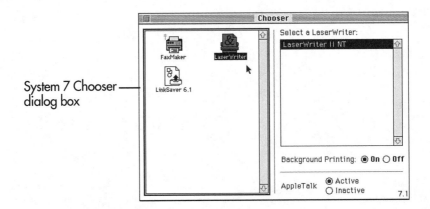

System 7 Chooser
dialog box

Each icon in the left half of the Chooser window is a *printer driver* (software that tells the Mac how to interact with that printer). Drivers for Apple printers are installed when you install the system software.

(In System 6, the drivers are called *Chooser documents* and are stored in the main level of your System Folder. In System 7, they are called *Chooser extensions* and are stored in the Extensions folder within the System Folder.) Printers from other companies normally come with their own drivers. The contents of the Page Setup... and Print dialog boxes will vary depending on the print driver you have selected in the Chooser.

After selecting a driver, you can sometimes set options for that printer. The particular options offered are dependent on the driver software.

Devices other than printers can also use the Chooser. As Figure 5.1 shows, my fax modem has its own driver (FaxMaker). To send a fax, I simply select the fax driver and then issue the current program's Print command. Instead of printing the document, the driver converts it to fax format and sends it over the fax modem. When it's time to print normally again, I just select the driver for my printer.

PROBLEM: When I open the Chooser desk accessory, I see other icons in addition to my printer. Can I get rid of them?

SOLUTION: Each icon represents a printer driver. If you don't specify a particular printer when installing the system software, drivers for *all* Apple printers will automatically be installed. Feel free to remove the drivers of printers that you don't have. Printer drivers can be found in the Extensions folder in the System Folder under System 7 or the System Folder under System 6.

▼ **TIP**

*As noted above, not all Chooser drivers are for printers. Be sure not to toss out drivers for electronic mail and fax-modems, for instance. (If you aren't sure what a particular driver does, return to the desktop, select the driver icon, and press ⌘-I—the equivalent of selecting **Get Info** from the **File** menu. You may be able to figure out what a particular driver is for or the program with which it is associated by reading the information in the Info window.)*

Printing in the Background

Background printing is like any other background task on your Macintosh. When it is enabled, you don't have to wait for your printer to print the current document before moving to another task. The system software and printer handle the data flow for you so that you can quickly get on with your work. This system software capability is only available for laser printers and the StyleWriter. It must be selected from the options available in the Chooser desk accessory.

Even if your printer driver doesn't support background printing, you can achieve the same effect with a print spooling utility, such as SuperSpool or SuperLaserSpool from Fifth Generation Systems. Print spooling utilities intercept all data on the way to the printer, store it in a temporary disk file, and then feed the information to the printer when the printer's ready for it—all in the background.

Not all programs support background printing. Desktop publishing programs, for example, often generate such huge print files that they are automatically printed in the foreground, in which case you must wait for printing to finish before doing anything else on your Mac.

General Printing Problems

PROBLEM: My printer won't print anything at all.

SOLUTION #1: The printer may not be ready to print. This is the most common cause of a printer not printing when you ask it to do so. Reasons can include:

- The printer is off.
- The printer is out of paper.
- The printer's cover is open.
- The printer cable is loose or is not connected to the correct port on the back of the Mac.
- There is a paper jam.
- The ribbon is jammed (dot-matrix printers only).

Many printers have one or more indicator lights that show whether or not they are ready to print. The light may be labeled "On-line" or "Select," for instance. If the light is not lit, the printer will simply sit there waiting for you to do something about it—like press the button next to the light to put the printer back on-line, add some paper, or correct an error condition. The type, number, and meaning of display lights varies considerably from printer to printer. See your printer manual for instructions on interpreting and responding to your printer's lights.

SOLUTION #2: The printer has not been selected in the Chooser. The Chooser desk accessory is the system software component that you use to tell your Mac which printer you want to use for the next print job (see Figure 5.1).

After you select a printer and specify options (such as background printing, whether or not the printer is connected over AppleTalk, and/or the serial port to which the printer is connected), all subsequent print jobs will be directed to that printer.

> **TIP**
>
> *If you have just installed a new version of the system software or have reinstalled an existing version, a printer is not automatically selected for you. Following system software installation, you should always use the Chooser to specify a printer.*

SOLUTION #3: The correct printer has been selected in the Chooser, but you have chosen the wrong serial port. Every printer must either be attached to the Mac's printer port (printer icon) or the modem port (telephone icon). If, after selecting a printer in the Chooser, the dialog box asks you to `Select a printer port:`, be sure to click the one to which your printer is connected. Selecting the wrong port will result in nothing printing at all. (Check the cables on the back of your Mac if you aren't certain which port is being used.)

SOLUTION #4: The system software may be waiting for an action from you. Selecting **Manual Feed** in the **Print** dialog box, for example, may require you to notify the system software that you are indeed ready to print. If nothing happens and you are not notified of a printing error, select **PrintMonitor** from the **application** menu (System 7) or click the **application** icon in the upper right corner of the screen until you see PrintMonitor (System 6). Once PrintMonitor is on-screen, you can insert paper into the printer's manual feed tray and continue, correct the error, or cancel the print job.

PROBLEM: My printer jammed in the middle of a large printout.

SOLUTION: Select the **Print** command and specify a page range that begins where the previous printout left off. The default (if you select nothing) is to print all pages of a document. To print only part of a document, enter page numbers in the From: and To: boxes in the Print dialog box (see Figure 5.2).

Figure 5.2

The Print dialog box enables you to print an entire document (the default) or a specific page range.

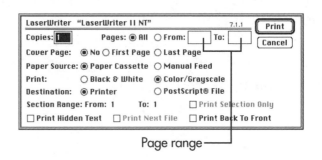

Page range

PROBLEM: My printout is too wide to fit on the paper.

SOLUTION #1: Print it in landscape mode (sideways). The Page Setup... dialog box (see Figure 5.3) has two icons that are used to indicate the orientation of the printout on the paper: normal (right-side up) and landscape (sideways). Printing sideways on an 8.5" x 11" page will instruct the printer to use the long side of the page as its top, allowing you to fit a lot more information across the page than you normally could.

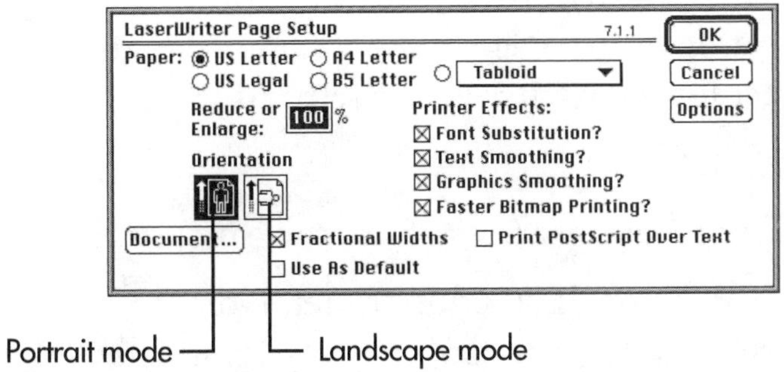

Portrait mode ⎯⎯ ⎣⎯ Landscape mode

Figure 5.3

The Page Setup dialog box can be used to set the orientation of a printout.

SOLUTION #2: In the Page Setup... dialog box, set the Reduce or Enlarge option to a setting smaller than 100%. Setting it to 90%, for example, will proportionately reduce the size of your printout to 90 percent of normal. (This option is only available for some printers.)

PROBLEM: I have two or more printers. How can I direct different print jobs to different printers?

SOLUTION: The printer that is currently selected in the Chooser will receive the next print job. If you want to send a job to a different printer, follow these steps:

1. Open the **Chooser** desk accessory.

2. Select the new printer.

3. Close the Chooser window.

4. In the current application, select **Page Setup...** and make sure that the settings are correct for the printer you've selected.

5. Issue the **Print** command.

PROBLEM: Can Adobe Type Manager (ATM) improve my printing?

SOLUTION: Yes, if you have a non-PostScript printer. Non-PostScript printers, such as the dot-matrix printers, normally create text printouts based on the same bitmapped fonts used to generate on-screen text characters. As long as you restrict your font selections to those font sizes that you have installed in the System file as screen fonts, the quality will be very good. Pick a font size for which you do not have a bitmap installed, however, and both the screen and printed output for those characters will be jagged.

ATM gives non-PostScript printers the same font-scaling capabilities as PostScript printers. When you select a font for which you have a PostScript outline installed in your System Folder, the characters will be created using the outline rather than the screen font. (The one exception is when you have the exact size of bitmapped screen font installed. In that case, the screen font will be used, since it already provides a perfect rendition of the font.)

> ### TIP
>
> *ATM can also be beneficial to owners of PostScript printers. Although it will have no impact whatsoever on printing, ATM will improve the screen display of any PostScript font by scaling it as necessary.*

Dot-Matrix Printer Problems

PROBLEM: My printout has large gaps between some words.

SOLUTION: Check the *print quality* that you've selected in the Print dialog box. You will probably find that you have requested a *Draft* printout. Select a better quality and try again.

Instead of forming characters from graphics (which creates higher-quality printouts on Mac-compatible dot-matrix printers), Draft mode uses the printer's built-in font. Although the printer prints quickly in Draft mode, quality suffers.

PROBLEM: At the top of the first page of my printout, the first row of characters or the top of a graphic image contains a single tiny vertical gap.

SOLUTION: Turn the printer off, manually advance the paper to the top of the next form, turn the printer back on again, and reissue the **Print** command.

When adjusting the paper, people tend to rotate the platen back and forth. If the last adjustment pushes the paper back *into* the printer rather than pulling it *through* the printer, the first pass of the printhead may be incorrectly positioned. On the next pass, the printhead will advance to the correct position, moving it a bit too far and creating a small gap or break in the printing. Since text is often printed with multiple passes of the printhead, you may see a vertical gap right in the middle of a row of text.

Properly positioning the printhead *before* you issue the Print command will eliminate this problem. There are two ways to do this:

- With the printer off, use the knob on the side of the printer to pull the paper through the printer. Be sure that the last adjustment you make before turning the printer on pulls the paper through the printer rather than pushing it in.

or

- With the printer on, press its form-feed button to advance to the top of the next piece of paper.

PROBLEM: Looking down the page, my printout has regular vertical gaps.

SOLUTION: On a straight text printout, this effect would look like you were printing the document double-spaced. Since Mac printers normally print using graphics mode, you will find that some rows of text are split in half.

Check the printer's *dip switch* settings. (Dip switches are tiny switches that are built into a chip. They are used to set the printer's characteristics.) You will find that one of these switches has been set to add a line-feed (LF) after every carriage return (CR). It should be set to No LF after CR. See the printer manual for the location and meaning of the different dip switches.

CAUTION

Never adjust dip switches while the printer is on! Doing so can damage the printer circuitry. Also, before changing the position of a dip switch, note its original position in your printer manual. (Printers designed specifically for use with the Mac will seldom require that their dip switches be changed from the factory settings, however.)

PROBLEM: The paper feeds too much (or too little) between pages.

SOLUTION #1: Check the type and size of paper that you have selected in the Page Setup... dialog box. How far the paper feeds when the printer receives a new page command is determined by the paper size that you have told the system software that you are using. Select the wrong paper size, and the printer will feed incorrectly.

SOLUTION #2: Check the printer's dip switch settings. They may be set for an incorrect page length, such as European paper. The correct U.S. length is 66 lines per page. A4 paper is 72 lines per page. (As noted above, do not touch the dip switches while the printer is on.)

PROBLEM: My printouts aren't starting at the top of the page.

SOLUTION #1: Each print job begins at what the printer and software consider the *top of form.* If you have reset the top of form—whether deliberately or unintentionally—the printout will start at the new spot.

Depending on your particular printer, you will use one of two methods to set the top of form:

- *Printers without a Top of Form button:* With the printer off, use the knob on the side of the printer to pull the paper through the printer. Stop advancing the paper when the printhead is aligned with the top of a page. Then turn the printer back on. *(Be sure that the last move you make before turning the printer back on pulls the paper through the printer rather than pushing it back in.)*

- *Printers with a Top of Form button:* With the printer on, use the line-feed button to advance the printhead to the top of a page. Press the Top of Form button to set the new top of form.

SOLUTION #2: Any *top margin* that you have set for the current document will force the paper to advance at the beginning of each new page. If you want to eliminate this advance and start right at the top of each sheet, set the top margin to 0 (zero).

Some printers may advance slightly at the start of each print job, regardless of the setting for the top margin. To see if yours does, turn the printer on and print the current window on the desktop (press ⌘-Shift-4). Watch the printhead to see if it immediately begins printing or advances slightly before printing.

PROBLEM: I'm printing labels and the printer is feeding too far between each label.

SOLUTION: The paper size selected in Page Setup... should be set to match the height of one label rather than to the length of a full page of labels. For printing purposes, each label should be considered a separate page. (To calculate label height, measure from the top of one label to the top of the next one.) The paper size tells the printer how far to feed to advance to the next label.

If your label, database, or word processing program does not offer a paper size setting that matches that of the labels you're using, check the program manual for instructions for defining a custom paper size.

PROBLEM: Some areas of my printouts are very light or blank.

SOLUTION: It's time to install a new ribbon. (The ribbon may be worn out.) Also, ribbons occasionally jam. If you don't notice it quickly, all printing will be done using the same section of ribbon. In addition to using up the ink on that portion of the ribbon, the constant friction can cause the ribbon to fray or tear. Even if the ribbon unsticks itself and starts to feed properly again, every new printout that coincides with the bad stretch of ribbon will be hard to read.

PROBLEM: Can I use my ImageWriter with an IBM PC?

SOLUTION: Yes, if your PC programs include a print driver for a C. Itoh Prowriter printer. Inside the case of the Apple ImageWriter printer, there is actually a C. Itoh Prowriter. As long as you purchase the correct serial cable and your PC software has a driver for the printer, there is no reason that you can't use the printer with a PC.

Laser Printer Problems

PROBLEM: Is it possible to do double-sided printing on my laser printer?

SOLUTION: True *duplex* printing (where the printer prints on both sides of a page without you having to reverse the paper) is a printer capability rather than a software function. Only a few printers, such as the newer Hewlett Packard Laserjets, offer duplex printing.

Otherwise, you can do two-sided printing only if you print the odd and even pages separately. First print all the odd pages, then flip the pages over and print the even pages on the reverse side. Some programs—desktop publishing programs, in particular—have print options that offer this capability. A utility called DynoPage (Portfolio Systems) provides two-sided printing capabilities for *every* program.

TIP

If you are going to use your laser to print on both sides of a page, be sure to let the paper cool before running it through a second time and use a heavy weight paper (at least 20 lb.) to prevent curling and wrinkling.

PROBLEM: I'm printing several related DTP documents. Why are the same fonts being downloaded to my laser at the start of each print job?

SOLUTION: At the start of a print job, the program checks to see if the necessary fonts are already in your laser—either because they are *resident fonts* (ones that are permanently stored in the printer's ROM, such as Helvetica, Symbol, and Palatino), because they are stored on the printer's dedicated hard disk (some printers, such as the IINTX, allow a hard disk containing PostScript fonts to be attached directly to them), or because they have been previously downloaded to the printer and are still in the printer's memory.

Most programs download fonts as temporary data. They disappear at the end of every print job. If you will be using the same fonts for several jobs, you can speed up the printing process by downloading the fonts *before* printing by using a special utility program, such as LaserWriter Utility (part of the system software). To download one or more fonts to a PostScript laser printer:

1. Run **LaserWriter Utility**.

2. Select **Download Fonts** from the **File** menu or press ⌘-**D**.

3. Click the **Add...** button (see Figure 5.4) and select the PostScript font or fonts you wish to download. If you are running System 6,

the font files will normally be in your System Folder. Under System 7, you'll find them in the Extensions folder inside of the System folder.

4. After selecting fonts, click **Download** to begin sending them to the printer.

The downloaded fonts are instantly available to any program that needs to use them and will remain in the printer's memory until the printer is reset or turned off.

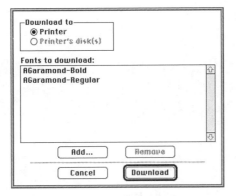

Figure 5.4

The Download Fonts dialog box.

In addition to downloading fonts, LaserWriter Utility can also be used to download PostScript files to the printer (see the discussion below).

PROBLEM: The service bureau that does our typesetting or printing says they want plain PostScript files instead of Mac documents. How can I create these files?

SOLUTION #1: If you are using System 7, you'll find this option in the standard Print dialog box (see Figure 5.5). If you select it, a new file will be created and saved on disk in the location (drive and folder) that you specify. No data will be sent to the printer.

If you're using a portable, saving a batch of PostScript files to print when you return to the office can be a good thing.

Figure 5.5

The System 7 Print dialog box has a radio button that you can click to create a PostScript file.

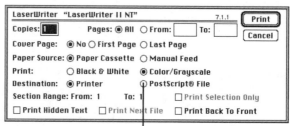

Select to create a PostScript file

SOLUTION #2: If you are using System 6, follow these steps:

1. Open your word processing, DTP, or other program, and load your document.

2. Select **Print** from the **File** menu.

3. *Immediately* after clicking the **OK** button, press **F**. If you were fast enough, you'll see a message informing you that a PostScript file is being created.

4. Quit from the program, and return to the Finder Desktop. The print file (*PostScript0*) will be in the same folder as the original document.

SOLUTION #3: A few programs—most notably DTP programs—have their own option to create a PostScript print file. Check your program manuals.

PROBLEM: Text or graphics are being clipped at the edge of the page.

SOLUTION: Your printer manual may not mention it, but lasers generally cannot print all the way out to the edges of the paper. The exact size of this "no print zone" varies from printer to printer. It can also differ slightly within the same *model* of printer. If you need a rough approximation, though, you can assume a no print zone of between .2 and .25 inch for each edge. Thus, to eliminate text and graphics clipping, be sure that you have set all margins to at least .25 inch.

PROBLEM: The spacing between characters on my printout is wrong.

SOLUTION #1: Turn off Font Substitution in the Page Setup... dialog box. If the current document is formatted with a bit-mapped font and you don't also have a PostScript version of the font, the printer will substitute a PostScript font that it *does* have—occasionally resulting in an odd-looking printout. Turning off Font Substitution will force the printer to use the font(s) in which the document is formatted, regardless of whether they are bitmapped, PostScript, or TrueType.

SOLUTION #2: Select a different font for the printout. If you format your document with a PostScript font that is built into your printer (such as Times or Helvetica), a font that you have a PostScript outline file for in your System folder, or a TrueType font, the printout will be formed from that new font—eliminating the spacing problem.

PROBLEM: My laser output is too dark or too light.

SOLUTION: Most laser printers have a dial that allows you to set the *print density* (the darkness of the output). Changing the setting changes the amount of toner that is distributed for each page. See your printer manual for instructions on varying the darkness or density of printouts.

PROBLEM: My laser output has white streaks in it.

SOLUTION #1: The printer is running low on toner. If your laser has a toner light, see if it is on. As you get close to the end of a toner cartridge, it's not unusual to see white streaks in your printouts (caused by insufficient toner). As a temporary fix, open the printer, remove the cartridge, and rock it gently from side to side a couple of times at a 45-degree angle. You can also adjust the laser's print density dial (if it has one) to its darkest setting. The next time the problem occurs, however, you should replace the toner cartridge with a fresh one.

SOLUTION #2: If the toner light has *not* come on, the printer may need cleaning. See your printer manual or the instruction sheet that accompanied your toner cartridge for cleaning instructions.

PROBLEM: Is it okay to use refilled laser cartridges?

SOLUTION: Yes, with qualifications. These days, many companies offer to take empty laser cartridges and refill them for you. Better companies will disassemble the cartridge, replace worn parts, and recoat the drum before refilling it. Refilled toner cartridges can often be purchased for about half of the cost of a new cartridge.

The biggest concern is that the refilled cartridge will leak and spill toner inside your laser printer. The resulting mess and danger (toner is a carcinogen) may considerably reduce the value of this bargain.

Whether or not you refill your cartridges is a personal decision. Since I don't share my laser and only go through a cartridge every three or four months, a savings of $40 on a refilled cartridge isn't sufficient for me to risk an expensive laser printer. If, on the other hand, you're using several cartridges per month (on a network laser, for example), savings from refills can be substantial. Before selecting a refill company, ask others for recommendations or request the names of several references from the refill company.

Special Printing Requirements

PROBLEM: How can I get my printer to print envelopes and labels?

SOLUTION—ENVELOPES: Addressing envelopes may be the last legitimate use for the typewriter. With the proper software and printer, however, even that task can be handled on the Mac.

The type of printer you're using makes a big difference in how successful your envelope printing venture will be. Printing envelopes on a dot-matrix printer, for example, can be an exercise in frustration.

Envelopes tend to slip about on the platen, so you may waste almost as many as you successfully print. Although you can buy continuous form envelopes that eliminate the slipping, they're much more expensive than regular envelopes. Slipping an envelope into the manual feed tray of a laser, on the other hand, is easy. If you plan to do mass mailings, you may even want to invest in an envelope tray for the laser.

Envelopes are easiest to print from dedicated software, such as an address book program (see *SolutionLabels* for some examples). Many of these programs also enable you to add graphics and postal bar codes to your envelopes. If you want to save money on software, you can design an envelope printing template in your word processing program. All you have to do is define a new page size that matches the dimensions of your envelope, and then create a template with a placeholder for the address. (If you don't feel like creating your own, templates for business envelopes in Microsoft Word, MacWrite II, WordPerfect, and WriteNow formats are included on disk in my book *The 9-to-5 Mac*, Hayden Books, 1992.)

CAUTION

Because laser printers generate a lot of heat, sheets of labels can only be fed through a set number of times before labels are in danger of coming loose inside the printer. Although twice is often the maximum, check the instructions that come with the labels.

*Before attempting to define an envelope page size, check **Page Setup...** for your printer. As Figure 5.6 shows, an envelope option may already be defined.*

Figure 5.6

Envelopes are standard page sizes in this Page Setup dialog box.

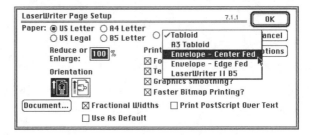

SOLUTION—LABELS: To start, you'll need the appropriate labels for your printer. Dot-matrix printers, such as the ImageWriter II, use *continuous form* labels (they have tiny holes along the edges that fit into the tractor feed sprockets on your printer). Laser and ink-jet printers use *sheets* of labels, which are generally more expensive.

Once you have the proper labels, you need some way of formatting the data so that it prints correctly. The best place to start is with your word processing or database program. These programs often include templates for printing several label types and sizes. If you don't find the template you need, you might want to check out a dedicated label program, such as MacLabelPro (Avery Labels), or one of the many commercial address book programs, such as InTouch (Advanced Software) or MacEnvelope (Synex).

PROBLEM: How can I print onto an unusual size paper?

SOLUTION: Some programs, such as Microsoft Word 5, allow you to define new paper sizes. Check your program manuals for specific instructions.

PROBLEM: How can I print the current screen or window?

SOLUTION #1: *Current window:* If you're currently running a program, turn on your printer and press ⌘-**Shift-4**. *Current screen:* Turn on your printer, depress the **Caps Lock** key, and press ⌘-**Shift-4**. (Note that neither of these commands works with laser printers.)

SOLUTION #2: If you're at the desktop and running System 7, you can select **Print Window...** from the **File** menu.

PROBLEM: Do I have to launch the program in which I created a file in order to print the file?

SOLUTION: No. Just select the icon of the file or files you wish to print, and press ⌘-**P** (or select **Print** from the **File** menu). Note that under System 6, you must select **Print** from the **File** menu. There is no Command-key equivalent.

The appropriate program(s) will be launched, and you will see the normal Print dialog box. After setting print options, the program(s) will close, and you'll return to the desktop.

Font Issues

PROBLEM: Some of my on-screen fonts look jagged.

SOLUTION #1: You have selected a font for which you do not have the exact size bitmapped screen font installed. Install the size that is needed.

Suppose, for instance, that you have set some text in 18-point Palatino, but you only have the 10- and 12- point sizes installed in your System file. The system software must then attempt to scale one of the installed fonts to make it match the requested size. Unfortunately, bitmapped screen fonts don't scale very well. Jagged characters usually result. Thus, one solution is to buy and install the exact font size that you need. See figure 5.7 for examples of an exact size and a scaled bitmap font.

SOLUTION #2: Install Adobe Type Manager (ATM), and restrict font choices to those for which you have PostScript outline files in your System Folder.

Times 72 pt.
Palatino 72 pt.

└── Scaled bitmap   Unaltered bitmap ──┘

Figure 5.7

The top screen font (Times) is based on a 72-point bitmap that is installed in my System file. The bottom font (Palatino) was created by the system software by scaling a smaller installed bitmapped font.

Rather than rely on bitmapped screen fonts, ATM will automatically take any PostScript outline file that you have and work the same magic on it for your screen that is normally done only for your laser printer. Regardless of the font size you select, ATM will scale it appropriately for your screen and make the "jaggies" disappear.

SOLUTION #3: Install and use the TrueType versions of fonts. Like PostScript fonts, TrueType fonts are infinitely scalable; they should look excellent at almost any size. Unlike PostScript, no special software such as ATM is required. TrueType font files are used to create both printed and screen output.

PROBLEM: I've formatted all or part of a document with one font, and the printer is using a different one.

SOLUTION #1: Turn off Font Substitution in the Page Setup... dialog box. If the current document is formatted with a bitmapped font and you don't also have a PostScript version of the font, the printer will substitute a PostScript font that it *does* have. Turning off Font Substitution will force the printer to use the font(s) in which the document is formatted.

SOLUTION #2: You may have a font ID conflict. Every font (Helvetica, HelveticaBold, and so on) is identified by an ID number. If two fonts have the same ID, the system software may become confused and use the wrong font.

Whether it comes from Apple, Adobe, Bitstream, or elsewhere, every font has a unique ID number. (Font IDs must be registered with Apple to prevent duplicate IDs.) When you install fonts into the System file with Font/DA Mover, conflicts are automatically resolved. If Font/DA Mover sees two fonts with the same ID, it simply changes one of them. System 7 handles font numbering automatically, too.

This problem can arise when you are using a utility such as Suitcase II (Fifth Generation Systems) or MasterJuggler (ALSoft) to store screen fonts outside of the System file. (Fonts are stored in documents called *suitcases* because of the appearance of their icons, as shown in Figure 5.8.) Although you can be assured that there are no conflicts *within* a particular font suitcase, there may be conflicts *between* font suitcases. To identify and correct this problem, each utility comes with a separate program that you can use to check for and resolve font ID conflicts.

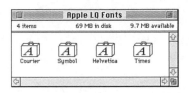

Figure 5.8

Font suitcase files.

PROBLEM: I have bitmapped, TrueType, and PostScript fonts in - stalled in my Mac. Which ones will be used *to display on-screen text?*

SOLUTION: The system software follows a predetermined order to decide which font technology will be used when displaying text. That order is as follows:

1. The system software first checks to see if you have a bitmapped screen font installed in the exact size that has been requested.

2. If the exact bitmap is not found, a TrueType version of the font will be used, if available.

3. If a TrueType version of the font is not found, the system software checks for the presence of ATM and a matching PostScript outline font. If *both* are found, a PostScript rendition of the font is displayed.

4. If none of these conditions are met, the system software takes the closest installed size of the bitmapped screen font, scales it to the requested size, and displays it.

PROBLEM: I have bitmapped, TrueType, and PostScript fonts installed in my Mac. Which ones will be used *when I print to a PostScript printer?*

SOLUTION: A predetermined order is used to decide which font technology will be used during printing. That order is as follows:

1. The printer first checks its own *ROMs* (Read-Only Memory) to see if it contains a built-in PostScript version of the font.

2. The printer then checks to see if the font is located in its own temporary RAM (having been previously downloaded).

3. If the printer has a dedicated hard disk, that is checked for the appropriate PostScript outline file.

4. The printer checks the *Mac's* hard disk by peeking inside the System Folder for the outline file.

5. The Mac checks its System file for a TrueType version of the font.

Moving On

In the next chapter, we'll look at video problems—difficulties with monitors, video cards, and related system software.

chapter **6**

Video Problems

In this chapter, we'll look at ways in which you can improve your Mac's video capabilities and examine some common monitor and video problems. Most video problems can be traced to one of several causes: program bugs or incompatibilities with your monitor or video card; incorrect settings in the Monitors control panel; or hardware problems with the monitor, video card, or cable. If your specific problem is not discussed below, here are some general troubleshooting techniques that you may find helpful:

1. If the problem only happens while running (or *after* running) a particular program, contact the software publisher's Technical Support department for suggestions or a software update.

2. If it's a general problem that happens no matter what program you're running, make sure that the monitor cable is securely attached and that the video card or adapter is properly seated in the Mac. (Shut down the Mac and turn off its power before doing this.) Check the monitor's external controls while you're at it.

3. Check the video settings in the Monitors control panel. You won't get glorious color if Monitors is set to display gray-scale or black-and-white, for instance.

4. Restart the Mac. Software-caused video problems will normally disappear. If a compatibility problem is suspected, you should also turn off all extensions or INITs. (If you are running System 7, hold down the **Shift** key while starting up the Mac to temporarily turn off the extensions.)

5. If your monitor came with its own software (many third-party monitors do), contact the manufacturer to see if you have the latest version of their software. (Changing to a new version of the system software—upgrading to System 7, for example—can sometimes create compatibility problems with video software.)

Monitor Setup and Expansion

PROBLEM: I own an IBM color monitor. Can I use it with my Mac?

SOLUTION: Yes, if it's a multi-synch or auto-synch monitor. These types of monitors can adjust themselves to almost any computer's video signal requirements. All you should need is a Macintosh video cable or adapter and an appropriate video card (or built-in video port).

The Mac LC can use a standard VGA monitor. All you'll need is a cable adapter. The number of colors that will be displayed depends on the amount of *VRAM* (video memory) that is installed in the LC. With

256K of VRAM, you can use 16 colors. It takes twice as much memory (512K) to handle 256 colors.

TIP

For additional video capabilities and monitor compatibility information, see your Macintosh owner's manual.

CAUTION

To be sure that you can use a particular PC monitor with your Mac, tell the dealer what model of Mac you intend to use the monitor with, and request the appropriate Mac cable adapter when placing the order. Some PC monitors come with a power cord that is designed to plug directly into a PC, rather than a wall outlet. In that case, be sure that an adapter is also included.

PROBLEM: I have a monitor that currently works in black-and-white mode. Can I get it to support gray-scale or color?

SOLUTION: The video modes you can obtain depend on the particular monitor and video card combination you have. The key is the monitor. Check its manual for supported display modes. If it can show gray-scale or color images, all you need to do is buy an appropriate gray-scale or color card. Some monitors, however, are only capable of displaying black-and-white images. Buying a color or gray-scale card for such a monitor would be a waste of money because it would still only show you black-and-white images.

QUESTION: My Mac has a built-in video port. Why would I want to buy a separate video card?

ANSWER: When you use the internal video port, the Mac has to use part of its normal system memory to display the video. Using a separate video card frees up that memory for other uses, such as running additional or larger programs. You may also notice an improvement in display speed, particularly with graphics-intensive programs. (Note that Quadras and LCs already have separate video memory.)

PROBLEM: I want to change the number of gray-scale or color levels that are displayed, but the Monitors control panel won't let me change the settings.

SOLUTION #1: The Monitors control panel is pretty smart. It won't let you select a color or gray-scale setting that your current monitor and video card can't support. It senses what equipment is installed and then determines what the allowed settings should be.

The built-in monitor of the Mac Plus, for example, can only display in black-and-white (no colors or shades of gray). In the Monitors control panel, *Black & White* will be the only setting presented. Similarly, an 8-bit color display card and color monitor can display up to 256 shades of gray or colors. The "millions" setting will not appear unless the Mac sees that you have a 24-bit color card installed or enough memory.

SOLUTION #2: If you have more than one monitor, the wrong one may be selected in the Monitors control panel. The selected monitor is always surrounded by a thick black outline (see Figure 6.1). Since each monitor and card combination may have different capabilities, different settings are displayed for each monitor.

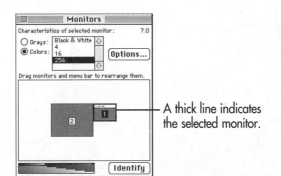

A thick line indicates the selected monitor.

Figure 6.1

Using the Monitors control panel to set color or gray-scale levels with two monitors.

PROBLEM: I just bought a 24-bit card and all my programs seem to be running slower. What's wrong?

SOLUTION: It takes more time for the Mac to move images at greater bit depths, so you can improve performance by setting the number of colors to 256 or 16, or even better to 1. Often it's best to do layout in the lowest bit depth possible to improve performance.

General Video Problems and Questions

PROBLEM: A program is telling me that it requires a specific video setting, such as 16 colors, rather than what I currently have set.

SOLUTION: The Monitors control panel is used to change color or gray-scale levels. Open the control panel and set your display options to match what the program suggested.

Some programs, such as games, go a step further and automatically set the proper color mode for you. When you quit from the program, it may even restore your original video settings.

> **TIP**
>
> *If you find that you frequently have to change the video setting, you might want to look for a freeware or shareware utility that can do this for you rather than using the Monitors control panel. Some examples include Switch-A-Roo and PixelFlipper. Some monitors (the ones made by Radius, for example) include such a utility as part of their software.*

PROBLEM: I have a 12" color monitor and some of my game programs don't fit on it (parts of the game seem to fall off the edge of the screen).

SOLUTION: Start shopping for a 13" monitor. Unfortunately, many games require a 13" or larger monitor. If you want to see the entire game window, you'll need a monitor that is large enough to display it. Before giving up, however, give the manual a quick skim. It's possible that the publisher has included a Preferences setting for smaller screens, or that there may even be a separate version for your screen size.

PROBLEM: If I look closely at my screen, I can make out faint letters or graphics that always appear in the same spot no matter what program I'm running.

SOLUTION: This phenomenon is known as "burn-in." Although there is no way to fix it, you can keep it from getting worse by using a screen saver utility or by turning down the monitor's brightness when you won't be using the Mac for an extended period of time.

Screen burn-in is caused by displaying the same unvarying image on the Mac's screen for a long time. In essence, the image is permanently etched into the video display.

Dimming the screen when the Mac isn't in use will eliminate the possibility of burn-in, but it isn't a very convenient solution—and it's easy to forget to do it. *Screen saver programs* automatically prevent burn-in. Whenever a certain number of minutes have passed without activity on the Mac's keyboard or mouse, the screen saver kicks in. A screen saver works by displaying a constantly changing or moving image on the screen. As long as the image continues to move, there's no opportunity for burn-in to occur. Two popular commercial screen savers are After Dark (Berkeley Systems) and Pyro! (Fifth Generation Systems). Each also works with Macs that have more than one monitor.

PROBLEM: The screen is black (no video).

SOLUTION #1: If you have a separate monitor (rather than a built-in one), see if it's getting any power. Check the power cord or try a different one. Flip the on/off switch to the opposite position. (If the switch isn't clearly marked, the monitor may actually be off.)

SOLUTION #2: Check the monitor's brightness control. It may be turned all the way down (which would make the screen black).

SOLUTION #3: If you have a separate monitor (rather than a built-in one), make sure that it's properly connected to your video card. A loose or damaged video cable or an improperly seated video card can keep the monitor from displaying *anything*. Remove and reinsert the video card or display adapter, and then disconnect and reconnect the monitor cable. Be sure to turn off the power first.

SOLUTION #4: Try the component swapping routine discussed in Chapter 1. By trying a different cable, monitor, video card, and Mac (one at a time), you should be able to determine which component is in need of repair or replacement.

SOLUTION #5: With older EtherNet cards, it's possible to plug the monitor into the D-connector. Make sure you're plugged into the video card instead.

PROBLEM: I own a Mac with a built-in monitor (such as the Plus, SE, or Classic). Lately I've noticed that the screen is doing odd things, such as fading in and out or getting very dim, or the viewing area seems to be getting smaller.

SOLUTION #1: See if this happens only in particular programs. If it does, it may conceivably be a software problem.

SOLUTION #2: Check the monitor's controls and make sure that they are set properly.

SOLUTION #3: There could be a screen saver installed that you don't know about. If the screen dimming ends when you use the mouse or keyboard, check for a screen saver in the System Folder. (If you're running System 7, look for it in the Control Panels and Extensions folders.) Monitor software sometimes includes a screen saving or dimming option, too.

SOLUTION #4: The Mac's power supply may be heading south (as in six feet under). It's time for a call to the dealer.

PROBLEM: The images on my monitor aren't nearly as bright now as they were when I bought it. (Or perhaps the colors don't look the same, or the viewing area isn't a clean rectangle or isn't centered on the screen.)

SOLUTION #1: The monitor may need a simple adjustment. Try changing some of the external control settings. (See your monitor manual for instructions.)

SOLUTION #2: Call your dealer or the manufacturer of the monitor. It may still only need a simple adjustment, but the control may be *inside* the monitor. Monitor repairs are best left to trained technicians.

PROBLEM: How do I get rid of that thin gray hairline that's a couple of inches above the bottom of the screen?

SOLUTION: You can't. What you are seeing isn't a defect in the monitor or the screen, so it can't be fixed. Some types of monitors are simply designed that way. Don't feel bad, though. It's a common way to construct a monitor.

PROBLEM: I've just run a program and now the screen is screwed up.

SOLUTION #1: The program has left the Mac in the wrong video mode. Use the Monitors control panel to reset it to the proper mode.

This problem shows up most often on color systems. In particular, running a graphics program or color game can cause this to happen.

Figure 6.2 shows an example of a "confused" screen that appeared immediately after I ran a game. All the icon labels look fuzzy and seem to have a fuzzy background. Another example of this is when the cursor highlight suddenly disappears or changes color.

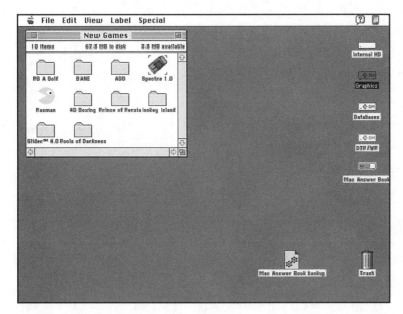

A "confused" video mode. (Notice the letters in the folder names.)

In any case, the easiest solution is to use the Monitors control panel as follows:

1. Select **Control Panel** (System 6) or **Control Panels** (System 7) from the **Apple** menu.

2. Select the **Monitors** control panel (shown in Figure 6.1).

3. Choose a different setting for Characteristics of selected monitor.

4. Reselect the original setting for Colors or Grays.

Switching settings in this way almost always corrects this type of video problem.

SOLUTION #2: Quit all programs and restart the Mac. Regardless of how screwed up the screen has become, rebooting should straighten it out.

PROBLEM: I know that the system software will let me do a full-screen black-and-white screen capture. What I need, though, is to capture only *part* of the screen, capture pull-down menus and dialog boxes, or do color or gray-scale captures.

SOLUTION: Buy a commercial screen capture utility. Most commercial capture utilities will let you do far more than the system software's built-in screen capture command (⌘-Shift-3). Most commercial capture programs can easily handle color and gray-scale captures, partial screen captures (including or hiding the cursor), and the capture of pull-down menus and dialog boxes. Three of the best commercial capture programs are SnapJot (WildFlower Software), Capture (Mainstay), and ImageGrabber (Sebastian Software). Each one also works with multiple monitors.

Unlike System 6, System 7 does support color screen captures with
⌘-*Shift-3.*

Two Monitors (or More!)

Perhaps you're asking yourself: "Why would anyone want two monitors?" There are several advantages to having additional monitors:

- Since MultiFinder (System 6) and System 7 both allow you to have several programs open at the same time, an extra monitor allows you to spread out your work. Which would you prefer as your office workspace: a 2' x 2' end table or a 6' wide desk? With two monitors, you can keep a word processing document open on one and a spreadsheet on the other, for example, cutting and pasting between the documents as needed.

- The second monitor can provide capabilities that your original monitor doesn't possess. If your original monitor is black-and-white, for example, you might buy a color monitor. Since a color monitor can display in both color and gray-scale, you can change its capabilities at will by using the Monitors control panel. You might also consider a full-page or two-page display as the second monitor, and switch to it when you need to view a large spreadsheet or do some desktop publishing.

- Finally, if either monitor goes on the blink, you're still in business. (You have a spare.)

QUESTION: I'm thinking about buying a second monitor. Can I use both of them at the same time?

ANSWER: Absolutely! As long as your Mac contains a NuBus or adapter slot, you should be able to use it to add a video adapter for a second monitor.

In fact, if your Mac has *several* NuBus slots, you can add additional video cards to power *several* monitors. (Most people, however, find that two are plenty.)

PROBLEM: My Mac doesn't have a video port or a slot for a video card. Can I still hook up an external monitor?

SOLUTION: Buy a third-party display adapter. This situation is most common with Macs that have a built-in display. Look through some Macintosh magazines and you're sure to find several companies that sell display adapters, including some for older Macs. Who says you can't connect a full-page display to a slotless Mac?

The instructions in ROM (Read-Only Memory) for your Mac, however, may limit the types of external monitors you can or should consider. The Mac Plus's ROM, for example, cannot support color.

PROBLEM: I just bought a second monitor. How can I make the Mac run programs from it, instead of using my original monitor?

SOLUTION: Let's see. Is this what happened? You just spent a small fortune on a two-page display to make it easier to do desktop publishing. Unfortunately, your DTP program is still loading on your original, small monitor. Even after dragging the documents over to the two-page display, the DTP program may not let you expand them to the full size of the new screen. And even if it does, all the menus are still stuck over on your original monitor!

The Monitors control panel determines which monitor will be used as the main monitor. When you open the control panel (see Figure 6.1), you should see both your monitors displayed and numbered (as *1* and *2*). The monitor with the menu bar across its top will be the one where programs will load and pull-down menus will appear. To change this, click on the tiny menu bar and drag it to the picture of the other monitor. The next time you start up the Mac, your new monitor will be the main monitor.

CAUTION

You must restart the system in order for this change to take effect. If you want to put this setting back the way it was, you must open the Monitors control panel again, drag the menu bar back to the first monitor, and then restart the Mac again.

PROBLEM: I have two monitors and I've noticed that the picture on one (or both of them) seems to be shimmering.

SOLUTION: One of the monitors may be causing interference on the other one. Try moving them farther apart.

PROBLEM: I have two monitors. Sometimes when I open desk accessories, control panels, or certain documents, I can't find their windows!

SOLUTION: You've probably changed the *startup monitor* (the one with the tiny menu bar across its top) in the Monitors control panel. Open Monitors and change it back by dragging the menu bar to the other monitor. Then reboot the Mac. Finally, reopen the DAs and CDEVs, move them to the current main monitor, and save (if the utility or program has a Save command) or close them.

Here's how this problem occurs. When you boot up the Mac, one of your monitors is the startup monitor—the one on which all program menus appear. The other monitor can still be used, but you must drag document windows to it.

During a computing session, let's say you've dragged your address book DA's window to the secondary monitor or perhaps you've dragged a particular word processing document to that screen. When documents are saved or desk accessories are moved, many programs and DAs keep track of window positions. The next time you open that DA or word processing document, it automatically opens in the spot in which it was last located. If you've since switched the secondary and primary monitors with the Monitors CDEV, those DA windows that were originally on the secondary monitor may now be somewhere off-screen and are, therefore, unreachable. Switching the monitors back again will let you get at these DAs.

Moving On

In the next chapter, we'll discuss problems that can occur with typical Macintosh *input devices:* the keyboard, mouse, and trackball.

Keyboard, Mouse, and Trackball Problems

Of all the peripherals you can connect to a Mac, the keyboard and mouse (or trackball) tend to have the fewest problems. And when there is a problem, it's usually easy to fix. In this chapter, we'll cover some common questions that you may have about the keyboard and mouse, as well as discuss the few problems that may crop up.

The Keyboard

For most Mac owners, keyboard issues are more often related to "how do I...?" questions than to troubleshooting. Things are further complicated by two problems:

- The existence of four different "standard" Apple keyboards (the Macintosh Plus Keyboard, the Apple Keyboard, the Apple Extended Keyboard, and the PowerBook's and Portable's built-in keyboard). Figure 7.1 shows each of these keyboards.

- The use of *ADB* (Apple Desktop Bus) keyboards and mice for the new Macs, and non-ADB devices for the older Macs.

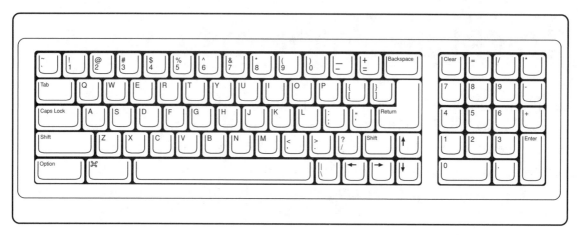

Mac Plus keyboard

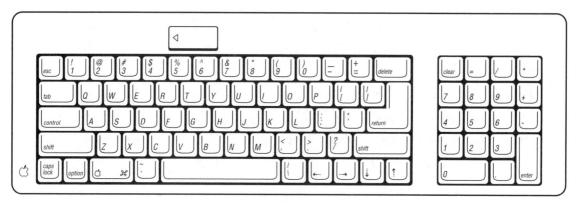

Apple keyboard

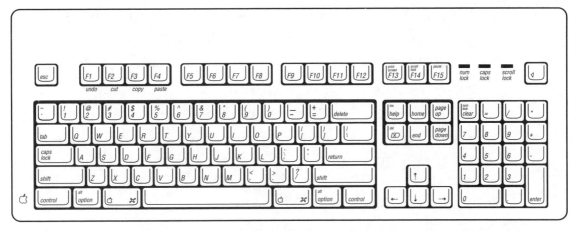

Apple Extended keyboard

Mac PowerBook keyboard

Figure 7.1

The four standard Apple keyboards.

Special Keys and Special Characters

Unlike a typewriter, the Macintosh keyboard contains a host of special keys. And what they do isn't immediately apparent when you first sit down at a Mac.

QUESTION: What purpose do the function keys (F1 through F15) and the other special keys on the Apple Extended Keyboard serve?

ANSWER: Any key that exists on the Extended Keyboard but is not present on all other Apple keyboards must normally be defined by your application programs in order to have any function at all.

Function keys. Of the 15 function keys, only F1 through F4 are predefined (as Undo, Cut, Copy, and Paste, respectively). The remaining function keys only do something if the program you're using has assigned operations to them.

You should note that function key equivalents for menu commands will not necessarily be shown in a program's pull-down menus. Pressing F15 in Microsoft Word 5.0, for instance, launches Word's spelling checker. Word's Tools menu shows ⌘-L as the only keyboard equivalent for invoking the spelling checker.

Home, Page Up, Page Down, End, Help, Del. If supported by a program, the first four keys are normally used for navigation. They allow you to quickly move to different parts of a document or worksheet without using the scroll bars. The use of these keys may differ from application to application. See the program's documentation. When defined, Help often brings up a help window, and the Del key deletes the character to the *right* of the cursor.

The Escape (Esc) key. Like most of the function keys, the purpose of the Escape key can vary from program to program. One of the more commonly supported functions of the Escape key is making its press equivalent to clicking the Cancel button in dialog boxes.

The Power key (open triangle). For some Macs (the II series, for example), this key can be used to turn on the power to the Mac, making it boot.

QUESTION: What's the difference between the number keys at the top of the keyboard and those on the numeric keypad?

ANSWER: Usually nothing at all.

Unless the publisher of a program has redefined the functions of the keys on the numeric keypad, a number typed there should be treated exactly the same as a number entered from the top row of the keyboard. Keyboard equivalents of menu commands, however, may work differently. Pressing ⌘-1 or ⌘-= sometimes works only with the number keys on the main part of the keyboard, but not with those on the numeric keypad (or vice versa).

QUESTION: What are the Shift, Option, Command (⌘ or) and Control keys for?

ANSWER: They are *modifier* keys.

When pressed in combination with a letter or number key, each modifier key performs whatever operation the system software or the programmer of the current application designed it to do. (To type a key combination, hold down the modifier key or keys and—while still pressing those keys—press the appropriate letter or number key.)

The *Shift* key is simple to understand. When pressed in combination with a letter key, it types the uppercase version of that letter. When pressed in combination with any other key, it types whatever is inscribed on the top portion of that key. Shift-4, for example, types a dollar sign ($).

Although commonly used in DOS programs (for the IBM PC or its clones), the *Control* key seldom has a function in Mac programs. The reason is simple. There is no Control key on the Macintosh Plus keyboard, so it's a bad idea for a program to assign functions to the key. You can create your own functions for Control key combinations using a macro program.

The *Command* key (shown as ⌘ or , depending on your particular keyboard) is frequently used to issue commands that you normally select from a program's pull-down menus. In most programs, pressing ⌘-S, for example, has the same effect as selecting the Save command from the File menu.

The *Option* key is often used to alter the behavior of programs, desk accessories, and menus. On a Mac running System 6, for example, holding down the Option key while launching Apple's Font/DA Mover results in the current System file's desk accessories being displayed instead of presenting the installed font list. With System 7, you can see an example of the Finder's use of the Option key by selecting the Special menu while holding down the Option key. The Clean Up command changes. The Option key also can be used in some programs—usually in combination with the Command key—to invoke some menu commands.

QUESTION: I need to use some foreign words in a letter I'm writing. How do you type foreign characters?

ANSWER: Unlike regular letters, typing a foreign language character always requires a modifier key. In some cases, a second keypress is also needed. Table 7.1 shows the necessary keystrokes for each character.

NOTE

Some custom fonts may not have all of the characters listed in Table 7.1 defined, and may substitute other characters here. Zapf-dingbats and several handscript type fonts are common examples.

Table 7.1   Keypresses needed to create common foreign language characters.

Character	1st Keypress	2nd Keypress
Ä	Option-U	Shift-A
Á	Option-Shift-Y	
À	Option-`	Shift-A
Ã	Option-N	Shift-A
Â	Option-Shift-M	
Å	Option-Shift-A	
Ç	Option-Shift-C	
Ë	Option-U	Shift-E
É	Option-E	Shift-E
È	Option-`	Shift-E
Ê	Option-I	Shift-E
Ï	Option-Shift-F	
Í	Option-Shift-S	
Ì	Option-`	Shift-I
Î	Option-Shift-D	

Character	1st Keypress	2nd Keypress
Ñ	Option-N	Shift-N
Ö	Option-U	Shift-O
Ó	Option-Shift-H	
Ò	Option-Shift-L	
Õ	Option-N	Shift-O
Ô	Option-Shift-J	
ß	Option-S	
Ü	Option-U	Shift-U
Ú	Option-Shift-;	
Ù	Option-`	Shift-U
Û	Option-I	Shift-U
Ÿ	Option-U	Shift-Y
ä	Option-U	A
á	Option-E	A
à	Option-`	A
ã	Option-N	A
â	Option-I	A

continues

Table 7.1 continued

Character	*1st Keypress*	*2nd Keypress*
å	Option-A	
ç	Option-C	
ë	Option-U	E
é	Option-E	E
è	Option-`	E
ê	Option-I	E
ï	Option-U	I
í	Option-E	I
ì	Option-`	I
î	Option-I	I
ñ	Option-N	N
ö	Option-U	O
ó	Option-E	O
ò	Option-`	O
õ	Option-N	O

Character	1st Keypress	2nd Keypress
ô	Option-I	O
ü	Option-U	U
ú	Option-E	U
ù	Option-`	U
û	Option-I	U
ÿ	Option-U	Y
¿	Option-Shift-/	
¡	Option-1	

TIP

Rather than refer to this table, you may find it easier to use a desk accessory to find foreign language and other special characters. The Key Caps desk accessory that Apple includes with its system software can be used to find single-keystroke special characters. You may be happier with a more powerful keystroke identifier, though. The KeyFinder desk accessory (part of Norton Utilities for the Mac) is an

continues

continued

excellent example of this type of tool (see Figure 7.2). Select any font that's installed in your Mac, and KeyFinder displays a table of all possible symbols for that font. Click one, and you are shown what keypresses are required to type that character. You can also copy and paste any character into the current document, just as you can with Key Caps.

Figure 7.2

The KeyFinder desk accessory.

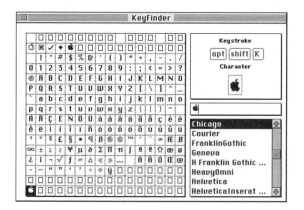

Some of the newer word processing programs include a KeyFinder-style utility. Selecting Symbol... from Microsoft Word 5's Insert menu, for example, displays a table of all characters for the current font. Click one, and it is automatically inserted into your document at the current cursor position.

Changing Key Definitions

System 6 included a utility called Macro Maker that allowed users to redefine the operation that any particular key performs. By using Macro Maker's "record" function, you could record a series of actions and then assign them to a particular key or key combination. A Finder macro might automatically close all open windows, for example.

Since Macro Maker is not supported in System 7, if you want to obtain this added functionality, you need a commercial macro program, such as QuicKeys 2 from CE Software.

Keyboard Problems

PROBLEM: Extra copies of some letters are appearing in my documents, but I'm not typing them.

SOLUTION #1: The Delay Until Repeat setting in the Keyboard control panel (see Figure 7.3) may need adjusting.

The Keyboard control panel allows you to set the Key Repeat Rate (how quickly a key will repeat) and Delay Until Repeat (how long you have to press a key until it starts to repeat). If Delay Until Repeat is set to Short, even the lightest pressure on a key can cause it to repeat. Choose a longer setting.

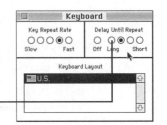

Figure 7.3

The Keyboard control panel.

Choose a longer setting to avoid extra characters

SOLUTION #2: Your keyboard may need some repairs. *Key bounce* is a fairly common problem among PC owners that have cheap keyboards. Touching some keys causes their character to repeat—whether you want it to or not. Happily, Apple-brand keyboards seldom have this problem. If yours does, consult your dealer.

CAUTION

Although you may be able to correct this problem by prying off the key caps and cleaning their contacts, most users will feel more comfortable leaving keyboard repairs to their dealers.

Dead Keyboards and Frozen Cursors

PROBLEM: The Mac doesn't respond when I use the keyboard (or mouse or trackball).

SOLUTION #1: You may be typing an illegal character. Press an unmodified letter key to see if the Mac responds. Certain fonts (most of them actually) have one or more undefined keys or key combinations. Symbol fonts, such as Zapf Dingbats, may have many holes of this sort. Pressing Option-Shift-C, for instance, produces nothing on the screen. Other unused key combinations in most fonts include ⌘-Option, as well as most Control key combinations.

The colon character (:) is illegal within file names. When performing a Save As... in a program, for example, entering a colon as part of the file name is often ignored.

SOLUTION #2: The cable for your keyboard (or mouse or trackball) may be loose. If the Mac doesn't respond to *any* character you type, the cable that connects the keyboard to the Mac may be loose or disconnected. Similarly, if mouse or trackball movements are ignored, it may indicate a loose cable. Check the connections. (As with any cable handling, it's best to shut down the Mac before tinkering.) If replugging the cable and rebooting doesn't make a difference, try a different cable. If your Mac has two ADB (Apple Desktop Bus) ports into which a keyboard, mouse, or trackball can be plugged, try the other port.

SOLUTION #3: If the Mac no longer responds to the mouse and/or keyboard, it may have crashed or may be "locked up." Such a crash is seldom accompanied by a warning or bomb dialog box. Often the only solution is to reboot, losing all work that hasn't recently been saved.

Sometimes, however, only the mouse will be disabled. You may want to try pressing ⌘-S (to save the current document) and ⌘-Q (to quit from the program) before rebooting. Even if the mouse is temporarily dead, you may be able to gracefully exit from open programs.

As a last resort, you can try pressing ⌘-Option-Escape, the emergency quit command. If it works, it will present a dialog box that offers the option of quitting without saving (see Figure 7.4). Any changes that have been made to the document since the last save will be lost, but you may find that other open programs are still functioning. If possible, you should save open documents in other programs under new names (in case they've become corrupted), quit, and then reboot.

Figure 7.4

The emergency quit dialog box.

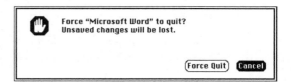

If you're running System 7, after rebooting, check the Trash for a folder labeled "Rescued Items." You may find some temporary files that, when dragged out of the Trash to a disk, can be opened and revived. Under System 6, the Trash will be empty. However, it's worth checking the System Folder for temporary files that your programs may have created.

Mouse and Trackball Problems

Since a mouse has always been an essential part of the Macintosh hardware, you won't have a fraction of the problems that you might with a PC mouse. There are no special *drivers* (software routines to make the mouse function) that you have to be concerned with, and you don't have to worry about software *compatibility problems* (the mouse working with some programs but not with others). Although uncommon, here are a few mouse problems that occasionally occur.

CAUTION

Lock-ups of this sort often indicate a software problem. You may have stumbled upon a program bug, you may have some incompatible software, or your system software may be damaged. If this happens repeatedly, refer to the general trouble-shooting techniques in Chapter 1 for help in tracking down the cause of the problem.

PROBLEM: Sometimes when I move the mouse or trackball, the cursor doesn't move, moves slowly, or is "jerky."

SOLUTION #1: The mouse or trackball may need cleaning. As it rolls along, a mouse collects gunk on the mouse ball and the rollers that surround the ball. Dust can also obscure the sensors that detect the ball's movements. Refer to your Mac owner's manual for specific mouse-cleaning instructions. These same instructions can be used to clean a trackball. Using a mousepad can help minimize problems of this sort by reducing wear and tear on your mouse.

SOLUTION #2: The settings in the Mouse control panel (see Figure 7.5) may need adjusting.

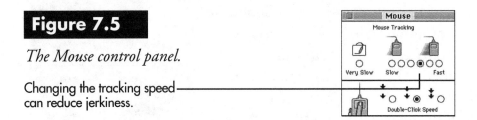

Figure 7.5

The Mouse control panel.

Changing the tracking speed can reduce jerkiness.

The Mouse control panel allows you to set *Mouse Tracking* (the amount of mouse motion required to move the cursor across the screen) and *Double-Click Speed* (how quickly two clicks must come together for the Mac to treat them as a double-click rather than two single clicks). To open the control panel:

1. Select **Control Panel** (System 6) or **Control Panels** (System 7) from the **Apple** menu.

2. Select or open the Mouse control panel. Each time you alter the Mouse Tracking setting by clicking a different radio button, try moving the cursor around on-screen.

3. When the setting is to your liking, close the control panel. Your changes will be saved.

SOLUTION #3: Get a mouse pad. If you're working with your mouse on a bare desk, the surface may be too slick to allow the mouse to roll smoothly. A mouse pad is the optimal surface for mouse work. (A trackball, on the other hand, isn't operating by moving it around on your desk. The only part you move is the ball resting in its stationary base. You don't need a mouse pad if you're using a trackball.)

PROBLEM: The Mac doesn't respond to the mouse (or trackball) at all.

SOLUTION #1: The mouse or trackball cable is loose. Like other peripherals, the mouse is attached to the Mac by a cable. If the cable is loose, the mouse may not function correctly or at all. After shutting down the Mac, check the mouse's cable connections to see that it is firmly attached. If the mouse or trackball is attached to the keyboard rather than to the Mac, you should also check the keyboard cable connections.

The best way to verify the cable connection is to unplug and then reattach the cable, not to just jiggle it. (This same technique is appropriate for checking any cable or card connection.)

SOLUTION #2: The Mac has crashed. Occasionally, the Mac can lock up, ignoring all your attempts to get its attention by moving or clicking the mouse. Before assuming that this is the problem, you should determine if the keyboard is still functioning. Try ⌘-S to save the current document or ⌘-Q to quit. If the Mac ignores your keyboard input, you'll have no choice but to reboot.

PROBLEM: What if I want to use *several* input devices (a keyboard, a mouse, and a trackball, for instance)?

SOLUTION It depends on the Mac, keyboard, and pointing devices you have.

ADB Macs   Newer Macs use the Apple Desktop Bus (ADB) to connect the keyboard and pointing devices. Each Mac has one or two ADB ports (see Figure 7.6). Many ADB devices have an additional built-in ADB port which enables other devices to be chained to it—much like SCSI devices are linked together. Up to three ADB devices can be chained in series from one Macintosh ADB port.

Non-ADB Macs   Earlier Macs (such as the Plus) are pre-ADB. They contain a single keyboard port and another port for a mouse or a trackball (see Figure 7.6). To connect a second pointing device, one of the devices must have an extra port.

Figure 7.6

Port icons for ADB (top) and non-ADB (bottom) devices.

Moving On

In this chapter, we've looked at common keyboard, mouse, and trackball issues. In the next chapter, we'll cover some of the meatiest problems you can encounter—those that happen while using application programs.

Problems with Your Program

Program problems are some of the most vexing problems you can encounter. They can result in lost time or lost data, and can be extremely difficult to diagnose. In general, the most serious program problems can often be traced to software *bugs, incompatibilities, design flaws,* and *user errors.*

A *bug* is an error in programming made by the person or persons who wrote the program. Bugs can manifest themselves in a number of ways. The most obvious type is a command that refuses to work at all or has some unintended effect. For example, if you issue a program's Save command, you expect that the current document will be saved on disk. If this doesn't happen or something else happens instead (the spelling checker pops up, for instance), you may have found a bug.

Not all bugs are catastrophic. If a particular feature doesn't work correctly, you may discover some simple way to work around it. Those bugs that *are* catastrophic (that is, those that can result in a system crash or lost data) may sometimes be worked around as well. For example, I noticed that whenever I ran a particular forms generation program, the system would crash shortly thereafter. The work-around I used was to boot the Mac, do my work in the forms program, quit, and then reboot the Mac. Although inconvenient, rebooting immediately after I had finished my forms work eliminated the crashes and still let me use the program.

Incompatibilities can exist between a program and your extensions, DAs, Control Panels, system software, or your particular equipment. Even if all problems occur in one program, it may not be the program's fault. It may simply be that an extension you are using is conflicting in some way with the program.

Design flaws aren't bugs. They're just bad programming. As an example, if you select a command and nothing happens, a program should normally put up a dialog box that *explains* why nothing happened. At the very least, it should beep to indicate that an error has occurred. Similarly, a good program should gray out any menu command or program option that is irrelevant to what you're currently doing. Unless you've copied some text or an object to the clipboard, for instance, the Paste menu command should be grayed out (made unselectable) because there is nothing to paste.

User errors are mistakes that *you've* made. Better programs try to anticipate and minimize the possibility of major user errors. Still, it's difficult to anticipate everything that a user might do. As an example, it's difficult to force the user to follow a program's installation instructions. If an important part of the program, such as the help file, isn't copied to the correct folder, the program may not be able to find it. The program may still run, but will probably display an error message if you attempt to invoke the Help command.

Troubleshooting Program Problems

The keys to troubleshooting a software problem are *replicability* and *isolation.*

- *Replicability.* Can you make the problem appear whenever you want? For instance, does it occur every time you select a particular command? Does repeating a certain sequence of commands or steps make it happen? Can you list the steps?

- *Isolation.* Can you determine under which conditions the problem will arise and when it won't? Is the problem with a particular program, or is it a "combination" problem that only occurs when you're using certain DAs or extensions?

If you can determine these things, you're in a better position to correct the problem yourself or explain it to Tech Support.

As mentioned at the beginning of this chapter, the usual causes of software problems are *bugs, incompatibilities, design flaws,* and *user errors.* Here are some steps you can take to determine which of these is causing the problem.

Handling Problems with a Particular Program, DA, or Control Panel Device

1. *To isolate the problem, see if it recurs under the simplest (cleanest) possible conditions.* Restart the Mac with all the system extensions turned off (see Chapter 1 for instructions). Immediately run the program, DA, or control panel where you experienced the problem and, as much as possible, do whatever you did just before the problem arose. If you can make the problem repeat under these conditions, you have eliminated conflicts with extensions, DAs, and other programs as possible causes. The most likely cause is the program itself (or one of its files), or an incompatibility with either your version of system software or your hardware. Work through the following steps to determine which of the problems suggested here is the specific cause.

   - *Check the manual for system software and hardware requirements.* You may find that it requires a later version of system software than the one you're using, that it does not support System 7, or that it does not work with one of your pieces of hardware.

- *Reinstall the program.* If the program or one of its important files has become corrupted, installing a fresh copy from your master disks will correct the problem.

- *Call Tech Support.* Since this is obviously a program problem, the software publisher's technical support people are in the best position to identify it, correct it, and/or suggest a work-around.

2. *If you can't make the problem appear under the conditions specified in step 1, restart the Mac again, but this time leave the extensions on.* Immediately run the program, DA, or control panel, and try to make the problem occur. If it does, one of your extensions is probably conflicting with the operation of the program. (See Chapter 2 for suggestions in handling conflicts with extensions.)

3. *If the problem doesn't appear in step 2, as much as possible try to repeat* everything *you did when the problem previously arose.* By this, I mean that you should run the programs that you ran before, use the desk accessories that you used, and so on. Sometimes problems are caused by a sequence of events or by running an ill-behaved piece of software *prior* to launching the program in which the problem surfaced. Some programs or desk accessories may corrupt the system's memory or leave pieces of their code behind. The *next* program you run may be the one in which you experience the problem.

Get on the phone to Tech Support or the publisher of the program, DA, or control panel that you believe is causing the problem. If it is indeed *their* problem, they are likely to have a fix or work-around for you.

4. If you haven't been able to recreate the problem, it's time to give up and go back to work. If the problem recurs, try the steps below or call Tech Support for additional suggestions.

Handling Problems That Appear at Random

In many cases, problems may not be easily replicable. Sometimes they'll happen; sometimes they won't. Frequently, you'll find that you're experiencing problems in *several* programs, rather than just one. The leading causes of unexplained and random problems are corrupted system software and viruses.

1. *If the problems still occur, use an anti-virus program (see Chapter 2) to inspect all of your hard disks for computer viruses.*

2. *Reinstall the system software.* The only sure way to correct system software problems is to reinstall a clean copy of the system software (see Chapter 2 for the steps).

Finally, if nothing else has helped, put on your thinking cap. Think back to when the problems occurred. Did those situations have anything in common? Are you only having trouble in communications programs (check your modem, cable, and the program setup instructions you've saved for the modem). Was a particular DA open when you quit from the program? If you can recall a common element, see if removing it has an impact on the problem.

Installation Issues

QUESTION: When installing programs, is it okay to bypass a provided installation program and install the files by hand?

ANSWER: It is safe to manually install programs only if the manual says so and if you know what you're doing.

There are several important reasons to use a provided installation program:

- The installation program knows which folder each program component should be copied into; you, on the other hand, may not.

- As part of the installation process, the installation program may create special folders or configuration files. If you do the installation manually, these files and folders will not be created, and the program may not run correctly (or at all).

- If the program has some form of copy-protection, installing it manually may make it unusable.

Note, however, that not all installation programs are foolproof. For example, installing some programs to a disk other than your internal hard drive sometimes doesn't work—particularly if the installation program needs to copy some files into the System Folder (which, in this case, is on another disk drive). In those instances, start by checking the manual. It may state which files are supposed to go where. If it doesn't, a quick call to Tech Support will usually clear up the mystery.

QUESTION: When I install some programs, extra files show up in the System Folder. Is it all right to delete or move them?

ANSWER: No. Many programs store configuration, preference, and other important files in the System Folder. When the program is launched, it looks in the System Folder for these files. If, for instance, you move or delete a preference file, the program will usually revert to its defaults. Any preferences you have created will be lost. Occasionally, however, these files are crucial to the program's operation. Without them, the program may not run.

Things can get messy when you decide to *delete* a program. Suppose that you've decided to switch to XYZbase and stop using Friendly File, your old database program. After throwing the program folder into the Trash, you pop open the System Folder. How can you tell which, if any, of those files were created by Friendly File and are now safe to toss out? Here are some hints:

1. Check the program manual. Sometimes it will list the names of the files that the program automatically creates and where they go.

2. In addition to looking in the top level of the System Folder, check inside the Preferences folder, if you have one. If the program is accompanied by an extension, a desk accessory, or a control panel document, you should also look inside the *Extensions, Apple Menu Items,* and *Control Panels* folders (System 7 users only).

3. Look for files or folders with names that are similar to the program name. In this example, *Friendly* or *FF* are possibilities. To determine if these or other files were created by the program, click on the file icon and press ⌘-**I** (or select **Get Info** from the Finder's **File** menu). Sometimes programs will identify these documents in the Kind line of the Get Info window (see Figure 8.1).

4. Call Tech Support.

Leaving these ancillary files alone, on the other hand, usually won't hurt anything. In most cases, they'll just sit there—unused and wasting disk space. Just be sure that you've gotten rid of any extensions, DAs, and control panel documents associated with the program. Executing them without having the program on disk can sometimes result in system crashes. (For additional information on system crashes and bombs, see Chapter 2.)

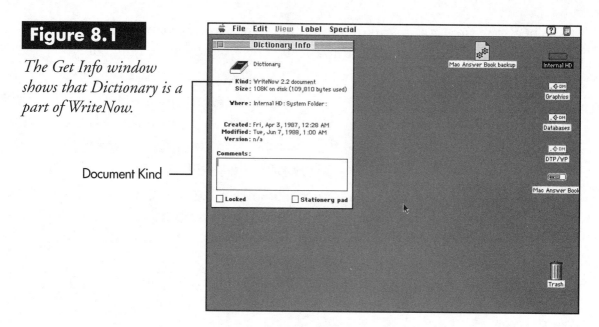

Figure 8.1

The Get Info window shows that Dictionary is a part of WriteNow.

Document Kind

Other Program Problems

PROBLEM: The Mac beeps when I . . . .

SOLUTION: The Mac beeps as a function of the system software or from a program instruction to do so. Unless the beep is meant as a notification of a process that has finished (a fax has been successfully received or an appointment time has been reached), a beep usually indicates a user error of some sort.

Trying to click outside of a system alert box, for example, often generates a beep. The system software is telling you that you must respond to the alert before doing anything else.

PROBLEM: I was in the middle of working on a document when the application unexpectedly quit.

SOLUTION: Allocate more memory to the program. This error message can occur when running MultiFinder under System 6. Normally, it means that the program has unexpectedly run out of memory and has been forced to quit. (Under System 7, a "Type 1 error" message—or some other error number—can mean the same thing.) The bad news is that any changes made to open documents in the program have just been lost. The good news is that you can probably keep this from happening again by changing the amount of memory allocated to the program. To change a program's memory allocation:

1. Quit from the program, if you haven't already done so.

2. Return to the Finder Desktop and click once on the program icon to select it.

3. Select **Get Info** from the **File** menu (or press ⌘-**I**). The dialog box in Figure 8.2 appears.

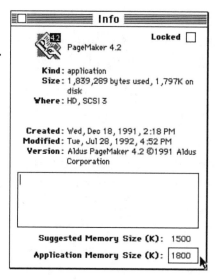

Figure 8.2

The Get Info windows for System 6 and System 7.

System 6

System 7

4. Enter a larger figure for the amount shown as Current size (System 7) or Application Memory Size (System 6). To start, you might try doubling the current figure.

5. Click the window's close box (in the upper left corner). This saves the change.

The next time you run the program, it will allocate the new amount of memory. If the problem disappears, you can try reducing the memory allocation to a more respectable level. If the problem occurs again, however, try some of the suggestions listed above in "Trouble-shooting Program Problems" or contact the software publisher.

PROBLEM: The program I'm running seems to be taking an unusually long time to perform some operations.

SOLUTION #1: Just as disk files can become fragmented, so can memory. As you run more programs, DAs, and so on during a computing session, memory is constantly being gobbled up and released. In the process, the memory for any particular program can become fragmented—broken into many chunks. This can result in a general system slow-down, as well as messages that there isn't enough memory to run the *next* program you try to launch. There must be sufficient contiguous memory to launch a program. Even having 5M of free memory, for example, won't be sufficient if it's divided up into bite-size pieces.

To straighten out this memory mishmash, start by saving all open documents and quitting from all programs. Then launch the programs again, opening the necessary documents as you go. If the slow operation hasn't been eliminated, reboot the Mac.

Having many extensions can also contribute to memory fragmentation. Try temporarily eliminating some or all of them and see if that has any impact. See Chapter 2 for instructions for dealing with INITs/extensions.

SOLUTION #2: Something else happening on the Mac may be stealing time from your application, causing it to slow down. Some background operations, such as text being spooled to the printer, or an INIT/extension constantly checking the system clock, might have this effect. Try running with all extensions off (or with the most suspicious ones removed) and see if the problem disappears.

PROBLEM: I have version 1.2 of a program and my friend has version 2. Why can't I read his files?

SOLUTION: New releases of programs are often *backwards-compatible.* That is, they can read files created with older versions of the same program. Where continuity is important, such as in word processing and database documents, most software publishers make an effort not to leave users with old documents out in the cold.

Older versions of programs, on the other hand, can seldom read files created with a newer version—particularly when a major new release is published, such as moving from version 1.0 to 2.0. The reason is that software publishers frequently add new features to their program. Microsoft Word 3, for instance, couldn't possibly know how to deal with Word 4 and 5's Table feature, since the feature didn't exist when Word 3 was written. Thus, new features often necessitate a new file format.

If you need to be able to read your colleague's new files, there are two solutions:

- Buy the new version of the program.

- Have your colleague use the new program's Save As... command to save his files in a format compatible with *your* version of the program, if such an option is available. (Both Word 4 and 5 can save documents in Word 3 format, for example.)

Just because a file has the correct icon doesn't automatically make it a particular file type. There are many utilities available that can be used to change a file's creator (the program that the file originated in) and type (the type of document it is: plain text, formatted document, or stationery document, for example). Although this can fool the Mac into thinking an Aldus PageMaker file is actually a Claris Resolve worksheet, Resolve still won't be able to read the file.

PROBLEM: I'm trying to quit a program or shut down the Mac, and it's asking me if I want to save a file.

SOLUTION: The current file has been modified since its last save. The program or the system software is giving you an opportunity to save those changes before quitting or shutting down.

PROBLEM: Why is this program asking me for a serial number again?

SOLUTION: The program has searched for the serial number and did not find it. Re-enter the number (it's usually on the disk label or in your manual).

There are many places where a serial number can be stored. The decision is up to the programmer who created the program. Three common places to store it are inside the program itself, in a separate data file, or in the System file. Replacing your current system software with a fresh copy will often result in some serial numbers disappearing. If the number was stored in a special data file created by the program, on the other hand, you may have moved the file to a different location or deleted it. The file may also have become corrupted, making it unreadable by the program.

PROBLEM: I've defragmented my hard disk and now one of my programs won't run.

SOLUTION: Some programs use a form of copy-protection that copies some critical data to a particular spot on your hard disk. If that data has been moved or erased, the program will not run.

Although most defragmentation programs make an attempt to leave copy-protection data intact when they reorganize a hard disk, they aren't always successful. To correct this problem, you will have to reinstall the program. (Note: Happily for Mac users, this form of copy-protection has virtually disappeared—most notably because of its potential to cause problems of this sort.)

PROBLEM: How can I combine information from several programs?

SOLUTION: The system software and provisions within some programs allow you to merge information from several programs by: *copying and pasting, exporting and importing,* using a *proprietary linking* procedure, and using *Publish & Subscribe.*

Copying and pasting. If you don't want to wade through program manuals, the simplest way to move data from one document to another is to copy it in the source document with the Copy command, and then paste it into the destination document with the Paste command.

Import/export. When you want to move a large amount of data between two programs, you may find Export or Import commands helpful. An Import command in the destination program is used to read files created in other programs. An Export command is used to translate the contents of a data file so that it is in a form that another program can understand. You may be able to import an address database from one address book DA to another, for example.

TIP

> *Some programs can read files created by other programs without using an Import command. Microsoft Word, for instance, can directly load MacWrite, MacWrite II, and text files.*

Linking. Some programs contain a proprietary linking procedure. You can use these procedures to create links between a Microsoft Excel worksheet and a Microsoft Word document, for example. Rather than recopying and pasting the worksheet information each time you change it, you can simply update the link. The revised data will automatically be inserted into your word processing document.

Publish & Subscribe. Finally, if you are running System 7, you'll find that some of your programs support *Publish & Subscribe.* This procedure is very similar to the proprietary linking discussed above. When there is a piece of information that you want to make available to another program, you *publish* the information. Then you open the destination document and *subscribe* to that information. When the published information is changed, the destination document can be automatically or manually updated.

TIP

Publish & Subscribe is particularly useful on a network for organizing projects that have multiple contributors.

PROBLEM: Is it okay to give copies of programs to my friends?

SOLUTION: That depends on whether it is a *commercial program,* *shareware,* or *freeware.*

Commercial programs that you buy from a dealer or through the mail generally include a *software license*—a statement of what you may or may not legally do with the software. Although licenses vary, typical terms include allowing its installation on only one computer or on multiple computers only if it is impossible for two users to be running the program simultaneously. If you bought a program for your personal use, the latter stipulation would allow you to install the program on your system at work and your system at home—since you obviously can't be in two places at the same time.

Generally, most programs are intended to be used by only one person. Thus, you should not make copies of these programs for anyone else. Unless they have also paid the software publisher for the program, they have no legal right to use it.

Freeware and shareware programs, on the other hand, may be given to anyone you wish. Both program types, in fact, *depend* on this method of distribution; that is, their authors *want* you to give copies away. *Freeware* is free software. Usually, the only restriction on distributing freeware is that the files must be copied in their entirety and left in their original state when distributed. *Shareware* differs from freeware only in that there is a price attached to the program. You are encouraged to "try before you buy." If you find a shareware program useful and decide to keep it, you should send the requested contribution or shareware fee to the program's author.

Moving On

As you've seen, program problems can range from inconvenient to catastrophic. There's nothing quite like a crash after you worked on a document for a couple of hours—*and didn't think to issue the Save command.* Because a program problem can have a myriad of possible causes other than bugs in the program itself, such problems can also be time-consuming and difficult to troubleshoot. If you follow the steps above, however, you'll have an excellent shot at identifying the problem and, conceivably, resolving it yourself.

In the final chapter, we'll discuss problems related to using a modem and telecommunications program.

Telecommunication and Modem Problems

If you attach a modem to your Mac, you can use it to exchange computer data over a standard telephone line. The word *modem* comes from the terms "MODulate" and "DEModulate," which describe what the device does. Computer data is *digital information* (patterns of 1's and 0's). Telephone lines, however, are designed to carry only *analog data* (sounds). When you transmit computer data to another computer, the modem modulates the data—changing it into a stream of sounds. When the modem on the other end of the phone line receives the data, it demodulates it—changing it back into digital data that the receiving computer can understand. The process of connecting two computers by modem over a phone line is commonly referred to as *telecommunication.*

Modems can be used to transmit and receive *any* kind of computer information: plain text files, formatted word processing or DTP documents, and even programs.

Selecting and Connecting a Modem

QUESTION: What is a "Hayes-compatible" modem?

ANSWER: Every modem has a set of instructions (commands) that it understands and responds to. Over the years, the instruction set designed by Hayes Microcomputer Products has become the most widely accepted and implemented standard for modems. Being "Hayes-compatible" means that a modem will respond correctly to any command from the basic Hayes command set. The advantage of owning such a modem is that you can be assured that any telecommunications program you purchase will work properly with the modem.

QUESTION: What is a *fax modem?*

ANSWER: A fax modem is a special-purpose modem that can send and/or receive faxes. Different fax modems have different capabilities. A few include fax capabilities only. Most, however, offer *both* fax and data modem capabilities in the same device. Some configurations you'll see advertised include:

- 9600 *bps* (bits per second) send/receive fax; 2400 bps data modem.

- 9600 bps send-only fax (no receiving capabilities); 2400 bps data modem.

- 9600 bps send fax; 4800 bps receive fax; 2400 bps data modem.
- 14400 bps send/receive fax; 14400 bps data modem.

This last example is the wave of the future for both fax and data modems. You should note, however, that *Group III* fax machines (the current standard) cannot communicate at speeds greater than 9600 bps. Currently, you'll only be able to use the 14400 bps setting with other fax modems that are equipped similarly. (When communicating with slower fax modems and fax machines, however, your fax modem will adjust itself to handle the lower speeds.)

QUESTION: How do I use a fax/modem with my Mac?

ANSWER: To send a fax with a fax modem, you open the **Chooser** desk accessory and select a fax driver (rather than a printer), and then issue a program's **Print** command. Instead of printing, the fax driver converts the current document into fax format, and sends it to the fax machine that you have designated. This means that any document you can display on-screen can be converted to and sent as a fax. The only big disadvantage of having a fax modem (as compared to a fax machine) is that the document must be in your Mac in order to be sent. If you have paper documents you want to fax, this means you must also own a *scanner* (an expensive peripheral that scans images and saves them as computer graphics) to get the document into the Mac for faxing.

Received faxes are stored on your hard disk. Most fax modems include software that enables you to view faxes on-screen. You can avoid paper waste by printing only those faxes for which you need permanent copies.

QUESTION: How important is the advertised speed of a modem?

ANSWER: That depends on how the modem will normally be used.

Modem speed is calculated in *bps* (bits per second). (Note: Some communication programs and modem manuals use the term "baud" instead of bps. Although they are actually different ways of describing communications speed, they are often treated as though they are synonymous. To avoid the technical complexities of explaining the difference between the terms—which, I suspect, wouldn't interest you in the slightest—it's simpler if you just treat the terms as though they are identical, too.) The speed that is advertised for a modem is always its maximum. For example, a 2400 bps modem can communicate at speeds of *up to* 2400 bps. For most modems, however, the advertised speed is not the *only* speed. A 2400 bps modem should also be able to communicate at 1200 and 300 bps, if the need should arise.

Some modems provide data compression—allowing two or even four times as much data to be transmitted per second, provided the receiving modem is equipped to handle the compressed data. *Throughput* (the actual amount of data that can be sent in a given amount of time) for a 2400 bps modem using quadruple compression is about the same as communicating using a 9600 bps modem without compression.

In choosing a modem for communicating between personal computers, faster is better. Faster speed equates with shorter transmissions, which is particularly important if you will be communicating at long-distance rates.

If you will be spending much of your time communicating with an electronic information service such as CompuServe or Prodigy, on the other hand, 2400 bps may be all the speed you'll need. Although some information services allow connections at rates up to 9600 bps, there is typically an extra charge for doing so. Browsing text screens at 9600 bps is a waste of money. (Incoming text that is scrolling faster than 2400 bps is impossible to read.)

TIP

If used carefully, a 9600 bps modem can be useful with an information service. You can log onto (connect with) the service at 2400 bps, make a note of any files you wish to download (receive from the information service and store on your disk), and log off (disconnect). Then switch to 9600 bps, log back onto the system, and download the files at high speed.

CAUTION

Even if the original PC cable looks correct (that is, the plugs fit into both the modem and the Mac's modem port), it is unlikely that it is the correct cable for a Mac. PC and Mac cables are wired differently, even when they have the same number of pins and holes.

PROBLEM: I already own a PC modem. Can I use it with the Mac?

SOLUTION: If it's an external PC modem, you can use it with the Mac. All you need is a new cable and some Mac communication software. If it's an internal PC modem, it won't work with a Mac.

As far as most *external* modems go, a modem is a modem is a modem. In fact, many modems you'll see advertised in PC magazines are also sold as Macintosh modems. There is no difference in their hardware. The only difference is the cable and software that are bundled with the modem. Your local dealer should be able to outfit you with the proper serial cable to connect the modem to your Mac. You will also need a Mac communications program; your dealer can provide that too.

Internal modems, on the other hand, are not interchangeable. The slots in a PC and those in the Mac are considerably different from one another. Thus, modem *cards* cannot be swapped between the two systems.

A few companies are now making Mac modems that connect to the Mac's *ADB port* (this is the keyboard or mouse port on most current Macs). Like internal modems, these units will only work on Macs, not PCs.

PROBLEM: I can't hook up an external modem (or any other serial devices), because I don't have an open serial port.

SOLUTION #1: Buy a switch box.

When both the Mac's serial ports (the modem and the printer ports) have devices plugged into them, the simplest solution is to buy a *switch box*—a hardware device that allows two or more devices to share a serial port. A switch box has a 2-or 4-position switch on its front; each switch position represents a different device. As an example, the first switch position could be used for your modem, and the second position could be for a video capture device. These are sometimes called A-B boxes.

Switch boxes only allow you to use one device connected to a particular serial port at a time. The switch only "switches" between the devices.

SOLUTION #2: Buy an internal modem.

If your Mac contains NuBus or adapter slots, you can use one of them to hold an internal modem. Internal modems normally come with software that fools the Mac into thinking that the modem is actually connected to the Mac's modem or printer port—even though it really isn't. You should note, however, that internal modems are sometimes more expensive than similar external modems.

PROBLEM: My telecommunications program is asking for a "baud rate" or "bps." Which value should I choose? What about "parity," "data bits," and "stop bits?"

SOLUTION: *Bps* stands for "bits per second" and is a measure of communications speed. (*Baud* is an older term that is also a measure of speed. Although the meaning of the two terms is different, they are commonly used to mean the same thing. When selecting a baud or bps rate in a communications program, it is usually safe to treat the terms as though they are synonymous.) In general, you should select the highest setting that is supported by both modems in the particular communications session. Thus, if your modem supports speeds up to 2400 bps but the other modem can only handle 1200 bps, you should both set your telecommunications program for 1200 bps—the highest common denominator.

TIP

As an alternative, you can both try setting your speed for your own modem's highest supported speed. Many, but not all, modems are capable of adjusting their speeds at the beginning of a session. When the modems connect, there is normally a negotiation phase in which the two modems decide what speed, error-control, and data compression protocols will be in effect for the session. (If speed is changed during the negotiation, you may have to change the bps/baud setting in your communications program to match. If you see jibberish on-screen, it's often the result of a mismatched parameter, such as speed.)

Parity, *data bits*, and *stop bits* are also communication parameters. As with bps, the two telecommunication programs should use matching settings for these parameters. Unless the other computer requires special settings, you may want to try the following ones to start (see Figure 9.1):

```
data bits = 8; parity = none; stop bits = 1 (or
"auto")
```

NOTE

The most common setting for stop bits is 1. MicroPhone II and some other communication programs also offer an auto setting that automatically adjusts the number of stop bits for different transmission speeds.

Figure 9.1

Here are the default communication parameters for a 2400 bps modem as set in MicroPhone II, a popular Mac telecommunications program.

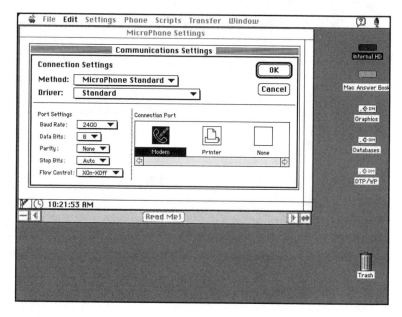

PROBLEM: What is *hardware handshaking* and why would I need it?

SOLUTION: Hardware handshaking is a data flow control technique which assures that the computer doesn't receive more telecommunications data at once than it is capable of handling.

> **CAUTION**
>
> *Using a 9600 bps (or faster) modem without a cable that is wired for hardware handshake can result in lost data or loss of the carrier signal.*

At transfer speeds between 300 and 4800 bps, most modems are able to manage the information flow just fine. A simple *XON/XOFF* protocol is automatically used by each system to tell the other when to start and stop sending data. At speeds of 9600 bps and higher, though, it's possible for information to be received so quickly that the computer can't keep up. To prevent this from happening, 9600 bps (and faster) modems should be connected to the Mac by a special hardware handshaking cable, rather than a standard modem cable.

The special cable uses one of its wires to implement an on/off protocol between the Mac and the modem. When data starts coming in too fast, the Mac uses the handshake line to tell the modem to halt the flow of data temporarily. When the Mac is ready to continue receiving, it issues a request for the modem to send more data.

Communication Problems

PROBLEM: The modem doesn't seem to be working at all.

SOLUTION: There are many, many reasons why a modem may not be responding correctly—including hardware problems with the modem or cable, and software problems such as selecting the wrong port in your telecommunications program.

First, check the modem's status lights. If they're all off, it means that the modem is off or isn't getting any power. Check its power cord and on/off switch, if so equipped.

If any of the lights *are* on, they should change and blink during a session. To see if the computer is communicating at all with the modem, start your communications program and type **AT** and then press the **Return** key. This is just a command to get the modem's attention. The status lights should blink in response to each character typed, and the modem should send an *OK* message to the Mac's screen.

If this test is unsuccessful, check the connections of your modem cable. Be sure that it is firmly attached at both ends, and that you have connected it to the correct port on the back of your Mac. (Some communications programs allow you to specify which port is in use. Others simply assume that you're connected to the modem port.) Note that PowerBook 100s have only one serial port.

Do you have the correct cable for the modem? If the modem has been packaged specifically for use with a Mac, the answer is probably "yes." If it was intended to be used with a PC, the answer is probably "no." Try to borrow a Mac cable from another user or a computer dealer, and see if there's a difference. *(Moral: All serial cables are not created equal.)*

Finally, check the modem manual for *self-tests* that you can run. Be sure to read the directions carefully for each test. Some require a loopback plug or connection to another system to work correctly.

Once you are certain that the Mac is communicating with the modem, you should determine if the modem can communicate with the outside world. As a test, you can use your telecommunications program to dial the phone number for the local time, for instance. To make the modem dial, type **ATDT** followed by the phone number and a semicolon (;), and then press the **Return** key. For example, if the number is 455-8200, you would type **ATDT4558200;** and then press **Return**. (ATDT tells the modem to dial using touch tones instead of pulses. The semicolon at the end of the number instructs the modem to return to command state as soon as it is done dialing.) You can listen to the entire conversation through the modem's speaker. Type **ATH** and press **Return** when you want to hang up.

Although these AT commands are fairly standard, the ones used by your modem could be different. If these commands do not have the proper effect, check your modem manual for equivalent commands.

PROBLEM: I've just connected with another computer, and my screen is filled with garbage.

SOLUTION: One or more of the communication parameters between the two systems is mismatched. Call the other person and agree on specific settings before attempting to connect again.

PROBLEM: I can't see anything that I'm typing, or every character I type prints twice on the screen (as in, HHii JJiimm).

SOLUTION: *Local echo* is set incorrectly in your telecommunications program. Try the opposite setting. Local echo governs whether characters that you type are displayed by your communications program (Local echo = ON), or whether these characters can be expected to be echoed back by the other computer and only displayed at that time (Local echo = off).

If you are also a PC user, you're probably more familiar with the terms "full duplex" and "half duplex" than you are with "local echo." If you are connecting to a computer system that uses full duplex (can send and receive data simultaneously), you should usually set Local echo to Off. If the other computer uses half duplex, you should set Local echo to On.

If it's obvious that you have the wrong setting for a particular session, you should be able to change it while on-line without affecting the connection. See your telecommunications program manual for instructions.

PROBLEM: Text that I'm sending and receiving is too long to fit on the line; that is, many characters are printing in the last character position of each line (at the far right side of the screen).

SOLUTION: Set **Auto Wraparound** to **On** in the communications program. This feature (or one with a similar name) instructs the communications program to do a word wrap automatically at the end of each line—just like a word processing program.

A similar problem can sometimes occur in which all text is printed on the same screen line—over-writing the same line each time. Look for an option in your communications program that allows you to add a line-feed (LF) to every line of incoming text or a terminal emulation mode that does this automatically for you. (A terminal emulation mode makes your Mac take on the characteristics of a specific telecommunications terminal, such as a DEC VT100.)

PROBLEM: I see a "No Carrier" or "Carrier Lost" message on-screen.

SOLUTION: The phone line connection between the two computers has been lost. Instruct your communications program to redial the other computer.

Many things can cause a connection to be lost. Common causes include too much noise on the line, mismatched communication parameters, computer problems (a crash, for example), or one user selecting his/her program's Hang Up command. In fact, you'll normally see this message at the end of every communications session.

TIP

If a connection is repeatedly lost, your best bet is to wait awhile before calling back (so line conditions have a chance to improve or you'll have better odds of getting a different line). If you see this message at the beginning of every communications session with a particular computer, your communication program parameters may not match, or your modems may be incompatible.

Phone Dialing

In addition to enabling you to exchange data with other computers (and use some of the popular information services), owning a modem gives your Mac a bonus capability. You can use a modem to speed-dial numbers in an address book program or desk accessory.

PROBLEM: How can I dial phone numbers through the Mac?

SOLUTION #1: If you've used a telecommunications program, obviously you've noticed that it's possible to dial phone numbers through your modem. That's how you connected to the other computers, bulletin board systems, or information services. The most practical way to dial numbers through a modem is by using an *address book program* or desk accessory. If you don't have one, you can use the Address Book stack that comes with HyperCard. First, however, be sure to run the Phone Dialer stack (Figure 9.2) to set your dialing options.

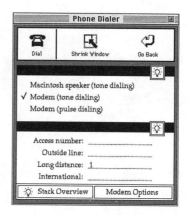

Figure 9.2

*Use the Phone Dialer stack
to specify dialing options to
be used by HyperCard.*

SOLUTION #2: The Mac's speaker can also be used to generate the touch tones needed to dial a phone. Using this method, however, is a bit inconvenient. You must instruct your dialing program to play tones through the speaker. Then when dialing, you must take the phone off the hook and put it close to the Mac's speaker. You may also have to increase the Mac's speaker volume using the Sound control panel.

PROBLEM: When I dial a call using the modem, I hear the other person through my modem's speaker.

SOLUTION: After dialing a call, the modem should be instructed to turn off the speaker.

Whether you will be able to correct this problem depends on the program or desk accessory that you are using. Better programs will allow you to send a command to the modem after dialing. For example, Figure 9.3 shows the dialing preference settings available for INtouch, a popular address book DA. The InTouch manual suggests using ;h as a dialing prefix. This command instructs the modem to switch to command mode after dialing the number and then to hang up. As long as you pick up the telephone handset before the modem finishes dialing, you should be able to continue the call normally— without interference from the modem speaker.

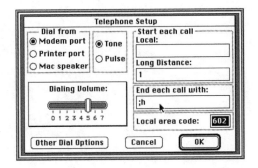

Figure 9.3

INtouch can be configured to turn off the modem's speaker immediately after dialing has been completed.

The End

In this chapter, you learned how to fix most of the common problems you'll encounter while using a modem. Be sure to check out the appendices that follow. They offer useful tips on selecting and upgrading your computer hardware, instructions on how to (and how *not* to) talk to technical support, and descriptions of some software tools that will help in your troubleshooting and maintenance efforts.

You're now well-equipped to handle your Mac when it misbehaves. When a problem occurs, just use the troubleshooting techniques described in this book. You'll save yourself plenty of time, money, and aggravation. (And you'll also have that warm, fuzzy feeling you get when you *know* what a problem is, and you have figured out how to fix it yourself!)

Dealing with the Dealer and Technical Support (Who Ya Gonna Call?)

You can't fix everything yourself. When a difficult problem arises, where do you turn for help? If it's a hardware problem (or you *think* it's a hardware problem), the place to start is with the dealer or mail-order company where you purchased the hardware. In addition to helping you diagnose the problem, the dealer should be able to tell you whether it can be serviced by them or if you should contact the manufacturer.

Software problems are another matter. If you're having trouble getting a particular program to work, the best source of information is the software company's Technical Support Department. (See "Talking to Tech Support," below, for some helpful hints.) Although you may avoid a toll call by contacting the dealer or mail-order house, their support staff usually won't know the program as well as the company that wrote it.

> *Bad disks are an exception to this rule. If you buy a program that contains a damaged disk, most dealers will gladly exchange the package or arrange for the software publisher to send you a replacement disk.*

Talking to Tech Support

Okay, so it's time to pick up the phone. The thought of talking to Tech Support can be intimidating, particularly if you're a Macintosh novice. Don't worry. Their sole function is to help. "Helping" may be as direct as answering a specific question you have or may involve walking you through a procedure. The support person's job is to do whatever is necessary—within reason—to resolve your problem.

What You *Shouldn't* Expect from Tech Support

Even if you haven't dealt with support before, you've probably formed some impressions of what it might be like. Everyone has heard the horror stories of being placed on "infinite hold," playing "telephone tag" for a week, or having been mistreated. Sometimes these things do happen, but the situation is improving. Most companies recognize that their image is on the line, so they adequately staff and train their support people.

As a former Technical Support Director, I know how difficult manning the phones can be. The following tips—written from the support staff's perspective—are general guidelines for the kinds of help that you should *not* expect from support, as well as some suggestions for what *not* to do on the phone.

- First, although you don't have to be a Mac expert, there are some things that the support person will expect you to know, such as how to start up a program, use the mouse, and load and save files. If you don't have the basics under your belt, you're well advised to run through your Mac owner's manual before calling. The support person's job is to help you use their program or piece of hardware, not to provide a computer literacy course.

- Second, if you don't own a legal copy of the program (a friend made you a copy, for example), don't call at all. If you haven't paid for the software, you aren't entitled to assistance.

- Third, if your questions are related to sales information (price, availability of a new version, and so on), features of the current upgrade, or the status of an order, you should normally ask to speak to someone in Sales or Customer Service. In most companies, Technical Support is devoted only to helping customers use the products. Tracking the status of an order is usually someone else's job.

- Fourth, don't give up too quickly. Wait a reasonable amount of time for a support person before leaving your name and number for a call-back. If the Technical Support Department is short-staffed, there may be precious little time for them to return calls. If your problem is urgent, it's best to stay on the line. If you *do* leave a number, however, make sure that it's one at which you can usually be reached—normally, your office number.

  If you're in and out of the office all day, don't even bother to leave a number. Playing telephone tag with a support person will quickly drive you both nuts—and probably make you both angry, too. Similarly, don't leave multiple phone numbers. Support people seldom have time to chase you. (If they do reach you on your car phone, chances are good that your computer won't be in front of you.)

- Finally, as a common courtesy, don't put the support person on hold. I know this sounds unfair. When you call, *you* may end up on hold for several minutes before connecting with a support person. Their job is to get on the phone, solve the problem as quickly as possible, and then move on to the next customer. Placing the support person on hold because someone important has come into your office or another line is ringing is likely to result in an abrupt end to the call. (You wouldn't ask the plumber to hang around on your porch while you take a call, would you?) Try to time support calls for moments when you are unlikely to be interrupted.

Preparing for the Call

With that out of the way, let's prepare for the call. To improve the odds of having your problem resolved, there are several things you can (and should) do beforehand.

1. *RTM (Read the Manual).* Common procedures and problems are normally discussed in the user manual. If you can't find a solution to your problem or if the manual's explanation isn't helpful, it's definitely time to pick up the phone.

2. *Have essential information at your fingertips.* Unless you've tripped over a program bug or just want to know how to use a specific feature, there is certain information you should have ready. Prepare for it, and you can often shorten the call by several minutes. These essentials include:

   - the version of their program that you're running (see Figure A.1)

   - the version of the system software that you're using and the amount of RAM in your Mac (see Figure A.2)

- the type of Mac you have (Classic, IIci, PowerBook 170, and so on)

- the exact wording of any error messages that appeared on-screen.

- your serial number if the product has one. (Many tech support departments will ask for it.)

Figure A.1

To find a program's version number, return to the desktop, click the program's icon, and select Get Info (⌘-I) from the File menu.

Version number ─────

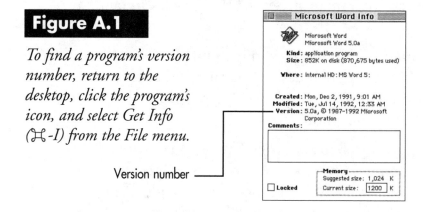

Placing the Call

Go ahead and make the call now. If possible, try to be at your computer when calling. If your problem isn't an obvious one with a simple solution, the support person may want you to try some things on your Mac while you're on the phone.

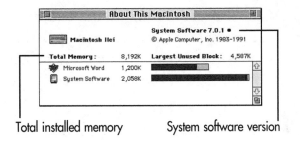

Figure A.2

To determine which System version you're using and the amount of RAM (Total Memory) in your Mac, return to the desktop, pull down the Apple menu, and select About This Macintosh (System 7) or About the Finder (System 6).

Just the facts, ma'am. When you connect, state your problem as briefly and directly as possible, such as: "Every time I choose a new font in WeasleCalc 1.5, the cursor locks up." The temptation is to recite a 10-minute diatribe listing everything you tried and the result of each unsuccessful attempt. Yes, you *can* do that. But if the brief explanation above happens to describe a known problem with a known solution, you'll have wasted ten minutes.

In general, most support people will want to direct the conversation—asking you specific questions or having you perform particular actions on your Mac. The more responsive you are to the questions and directions, the quicker the problem can be resolved.

Keep your cool. It's sometimes tempting to use a support call as an opportunity to vent frustration and anger—don't. (Besides, your anger is misdirected. The support person and programmer are generally two different people.) Don't get mad at the person who is trying to help you.

"But I don't understand." During the conversation, it's perfectly acceptable to say that you don't understand something that's being discussed. Because of their in-depth product knowledge, support people can occasionally lapse into a "techier-than-thou" monologue. They also may misjudge your level of Mac expertise. If their explanations or questions go over your head, it's up to you to tell them.

Other Ways to Get Support

If a product or an upgrade has just shipped or the company has few support people, it can be extremely difficult to get through to Tech Support. If your problem isn't urgent, there are other routes that you may want to consider.

1. *Fax.* If the company's fax number is listed in the manual, you can fax them a detailed description of your problem. Some of the larger companies also have a "fax-back" support service. You call an automated system and order particular support documents by pressing numbers on your telephone keypad. After hanging up,

the documents will be faxed to you—usually at the software or hardware company's expense.

2. *Company BBS.* Some Mac companies maintain a support *BBS* (bulletin board system). If you have a modem, you can log onto the BBS, download technical notes and program patches, and leave messages for technical support.

3. *Electronic mail.* Many companies also have support forums on major information services, such as GEnie, CompuServe, America Online, and AppleLink. Although a modem and an account is required (the information services aren't free), you may be able to get a quick answer to your question by leaving a message on one of these services. (Of course you'll need to be a member of the service.)

4. *Regular mail.* Consider this a last resort. Unless the support department is well-staffed, mail is often given lower priority than a phone call, fax, or modem contact.

5. *Support contracts and 900 numbers.* Some companies offer two or more *levels* of support. If you anticipate frequent problems or need preferential treatment, you may want to investigate the availability of a support contract or a 900-number service (so many dollars per minute or per call). Support contracts may also include one or more free upgrades to the product, making them good values even if you seldom use the support line.

Troubleshooting Tools

Prime requisites for successful troubleshooting are keeping a level head and attacking each new problem methodically. However, there are many problems which can be diagnosed easily with current software utilities. Having the proper tools can save you hours of aggravation and can help you diagnose and correct many common problems. Although there are other utilities you may want to consider, here are a few of the market leaders. Most of these programs should be readily available from local software dealers and mail-order houses.

Programs designated as "shareware" or "freeware" are available from user groups, information services, BBSs, and publishers of Mac shareware/freeware catalogs.

Hard Disk Setup Utilities

Hard disk setup programs provide essential functions such as formatting, partitioning, and testing hard disks.

HD SC Setup (Apple Computer, Inc.)   This program is included as part of the system software. It allows you to test, format, partition, and update the drivers for any disk sold by Apple Computer.

If your hard disk is Apple-made, you do not need an extra hard disk utility program. If you buy a non-Apple hard disk, it will usually come with its own setup program. However, you may prefer to use a different, third-party program; sometimes these offer more features and an easier-to-use interface.

DiskMaker (Golden Triangle)   If your non-Apple hard disk didn't come with its own formatting and testing program, DiskMaker is an excellent choice. It's easy to use and contains options for formatting, testing, partitioning, and installing new drivers for most hard disk brands.

Disk Manager Mac (Ontrack Computer Systems)   This program is frequently bundled with third-party hard disks, and performs functions similar to HD SC Setup. In addition to the usual formatting, partitioning, and testing functions, Disk Manager Mac can also park disks (safely position the read/write heads in preparation for moving the hard disk to a new location).

Hard Disk Tune-Up Software

If you have a hard disk connected to your Mac, you should consider buying one of the following utility packages. Regular testing and defragmenting is essential to your hard disk's health, and you will find the included file utilities indispensable.

911 Utilities (Microcom)   Complete Undelete, 911's undelete utility, is my favorite. Not only does it show you the percentage of each file that is recoverable, but it will also let you peek inside a deleted file and examine its text. It includes an exceptional troubleshooting guide, but it is currently geared to System 6 problems.

Central Point MacTools (Central Point Software)   Formerly called MacTools Deluxe, it—like the other hard disk tune-up packages—gets bigger, more flexible, and more powerful with each release. Version 2 performs hard disk analysis and repair, data recovery, backups, virus protection and eradication, and disk optimization.

Disk First Aid (Apple Computer, Inc.)   Although not the most powerful hard disk utility around, you already own a copy of it—it is included as part of all system software releases. Disk First Aid is useful for diagnosing and repairing disk catalog problems.

Norton Utilities for the Macintosh (Symantec Corporation)   Norton Utilities is an excellent package of programs for keeping your hard disk in top-notch condition. Norton Disk Doctor performs a general diagnostic scan of any attached disk, and can repair catalogs, check the boot blocks, and correct minor file problems. The program is simple enough to be used by novices. Other components of the package include a disk optimizer (defragmentation), floppy formatting utility, backup program, encryption utility, and programs to help recover deleted files and crashed or reformatted hard disks. Also included is the KeyFinder desk accessory, an extremely useful utility that shows you every character available in every installed font.

Public Utilities (Fifth Generation Systems)   This package is still under development, but should offer features similar to those provided in Norton Utilities and Central Point MacTools.

Hardware Troubleshooting Tools

There are precious few hardware diagnostic tools for the Mac. If you're repair service shy, a good diagnostic tool will let you know what—if anything—is wrong with your hardware and give you some idea of the size of the repair bill you're looking at.

Snooper (Maxa Corporation)   Problems with hardware can be especially difficult to diagnose. Determining that there's something wrong with the SCSI chain, for instance, can save you hours of fruitlessly attempting to locate what you think is a software problem.

Snooper is available in two versions: software only and software plus a NuBus card. The NuBus card (for slotted Macs only) checks the power supply, the system clock, bus activity, and the ADB data and power lines. The Snooper program runs diagnostics on the internal and attached hardware, including memory, mouse, keyboard, clock, math coprocessor, audio, video, serial ports, SCSI, and floppy disks. The software also calculates benchmarks covering the CPU speed, math calculations, memory, and video performance. (If you perform the benchmarks on a regular basis, you can compare performance over time and determine if part of the Mac is degrading.)

If you are charged with caring for several Macs, the entire package is a "must buy." If you're only worried about your own Mac, consider buying just the software.

Software Troubleshooting Tools

Help! (Teknosys)   Help! is a utility program that checks all programs on your hard disks, and reports incompatibilities, improperly installed software, and duplicate copies of programs. Help! contains an enormous database of compatibility information that has been provided by Macintosh software publishers. If there is a known INIT/extension conflict for a program or an incompatibility with a particular version of system software, Help! will point it out. Help! can check your programs based on the current version of system software that you're using, or it can perform simulations and point out problems you are likely to encounter if you upgrade to a newer version of system software.

Help! is most useful to individuals who are in charge of in-house computer support. To maintain the program's usefulness, you should subscribe to the update program.

Extension Managers

An extension manager enables you to selectively include and exclude extensions/INITs during any computing session. Normally you have to do this by manually dragging the extensions into or out of your System Folder. An extension manager can also be extremely helpful when testing for conflicts between extensions or between extensions and programs.

Extension Manager (Apple Computer, Inc.) (freeware)   Extension Manager can be found on most information services or obtained from a user group. It's more difficult to use than the other two utilities, but it *is* free.

INITPicker (Microseeds Publishing)   An extension manager that enables you to create sets of extensions for different purposes, change their loading order, and keep a log of extension activity.

StartUp Manager (part of the NOW Utilities from NOW Software) Simple-to-use control panel device that enables you to specify groups of startup extensions and CDEVs, and create a system profile report (useful when chatting with tech support personnel).

Heap Adjustment Utilities

In System 6, unexplained crashes and other memory-related problems are frequently a result of insufficient heap space. The following utilities enable you to eliminate heap problems by increasing or decreasing the size of the system heap as needed.

Heap Fixer (CE Software)   Heap Fixer is frequently included along with other programs sold by CE Software. It is relatively easy to use, and is most appropriate for individuals who have fairly static systems.

HeapTool (shareware)   HeapTool is extremely easy to use, and is well-suited to individuals who make frequent changes to their system.

SCSI Utilities

Hard drives and scanners are normally connected in series to the Mac's SCSI (Small Computer System Interface) port. Since each SCSI device must have a unique ID number, you can use either of the following utilities to determine which IDs have already been assigned and which ones are free. You can also use them to mount removable hard disks on the desktop.

SCSI Tools (shareware)   SCSI Tools is a CDEV that can be used to mount recalcitrant devices, such as removable hard disks. It also shows you which SCSI IDs are currently in use and which ones can be assigned to new devices.

SCSI Probe (SyQuest Corporation) (freeware)   Consider SCSI Probe, a slightly more sophisticated version of SCSI Tools. In addition to SCSI Tools' features, it shows the specific device assigned to each SCSI ID. It also enables you to password-protect selected devices and to specify a period that the Mac will wait at startup before attempting to mount the drive.

Backup Programs

When an important file disappears or becomes damaged, you have to either reconstruct the information from memory or a printout, or restore the file from another copy on disk. Since it's easy to forget to back up your data, a backup program formalizes the process for you. If you back up using a tape drive, the backup program can even auto-mate the process for you—setting the system to automatically back up at a particular time each day. A good backup system is essential for recovering from hard disk tragedies.

DiskFit Pro (Dantz Development)   An easy-to-use backup program. It can only back up to Finder-mountable devices, such as floppies and removable hard disks.

Fastback II (Fifth Generation Systems)   Powerful backup and archiving program. Supports many backup devices, including those that are not mountable, such as proprietary tape drives.

Redux (Microseeds Publishing)   Backup program similar to DiskFit Pro. Designed for Finder-mountable media only.

Retrospect (Dantz Development)   Powerful backup and archiving program. Supports many backup devices, including those that are not mountable, such as proprietary tape drives.

File Compression Utilities

Although hard disks have come down in price, they're still not cheap. One way to reclaim some disk space is by shrinking seldom-used programs and files using a compression utility. Compression programs are also very useful if you do any telecommunicating with other computers. Since a compressed file is smaller than the original file, it will transmit much faster, resulting in long-distance savings.

Compact Pro (shareware)   Compact Pro is an inexpensive shareware compression utility. Although it only runs as a stand-alone program (making it a little less convenient than the commercial programs), it does an excellent job of compressing files, and will let you divide a group of files automatically across as many floppies as needed. Highly recommended.

DiskDoubler and *AutoDoubler* (Fifth Generation Systems)   Different compression utilities for different needs. DiskDoubler is a stand-alone compression/decompression utility. AutoDoubler is for users who need automatic and on-the-fly compression.

287

More Disk Space (Alysis)   Automatic compression utility. Compresses entire hard disks in the background and decompresses files on the fly.

StuffIt Deluxe (Aladdin Systems)   StuffIt Deluxe got its start as a widely used shareware program. It is now one of the most popular compression utilities around.

Anti-Virus Utilities

Computer viruses are like infectious diseases. Undiscovered and untreated, they can lead to data loss and corrupted programs. The following utilities can be used to check disks for viruses and, in many cases, remove any viruses that are found.

Disinfectant (freeware)   This free, stand-alone, anti-virus program is available through the usual sources. It does not contain an INIT or CDEV, so it lacks the automatic file- and program-checking capabilities of its commercial cousins. It's still extremely useful, though. Watch the information services for updates as they're released.

Rival (Microseeds Publishing)   Unlike the other anti-virus utilities, Rival runs entirely from a CDEV/INIT combination, while providing both virus detection and eradication.

Virex (Microcom)   Virex combines an extension/CDEV and a program to provide complete virus detection and eradication capabilities.

Miscellaneous Utilities

The programs and INITs/extensions listed below are a grab bag of other utilities you may find useful. (In case you've already forgotten, an INIT—called an extension in System 7—is a small program that automatically runs each time you start up the Mac. Usually, INITs are designed to supplement the system software, or they provide a function that needs to be constantly available regardless of what the Mac is currently doing, such as the ability to receive a fax or execute a macro command.)

Adobe Type Manager (Adobe)   Adobe Type Manager (ATM) is an INIT that enables the system software to create scaled screen fonts from PostScript outline font files instead of using bitmapped fonts. Also provides non-PostScript printers with the ability to use PostScript outline font files.

After Dark and *More After Dark* (Berkeley Systems)   After Dark (the base program) is a modular screen-saving INIT. More After Dark provides additional screen-saver modules for users who want greater variety.

CanOpener 2 (Abbott Systems)   The perfect utility for peeking into files and examining the text and graphics they contain. Excellent for recovering data from files that can't be opened by any other means.

Macro Maker (Apple Computer)   A macro utility included as part of System 6. Not supported in System 7.

MasterJuggler (Fifth Generation Systems)   Utility for managing fonts, DAs, and sounds.

MODE32 (Connectix Corporation) (freeware)   MODE32 allows some older Macs (II, IIx, IIcx, and SE/30) to support 32-bit addressing, letting them use more than 8M of RAM. If you have an even older Mac, this utility will be useless to you. Similarly, newer Macs are already 32-bit capable, so MODE32 isn't required. You can obtain a free copy of this utility through most information services and user groups.

Pyro! (Fifth Generation Systems)   Solid screen-saving INIT with flexible options. Not as many modules as After Dark.

QuicKeys 2 (CE Software)   A general-purpose macro utility for System 6 or 7 users.

Suitcase II (Fifth Generation Systems)   Desk accessory/INIT for managing fonts, DAs, and sounds.

SuperSpool and *SuperLaserSpool* (Fifth Generation Systems)   Print spooling utilities for dot-matrix (SuperSpool) and laser printers (SuperLaserSpool) that enable your printer to print in the background while you go on with your work.

Index

HD SC Setup (Apple Computer, Inc.), 87, 89, 279
heap
   adjustment programs, 61, 285
   system space, 60
Heap Fixer (CE Software), 61, 285
HeapTool (shareware), 61, 285
help
   900 numbers, 277
   Balloon Help, 39
   BBSs, company-maintained, 277
   electronic mail, support forums, 277
   faxing problems to companies, 276-277
   hardware, 269
   mail, 277
   support contracts, 277
   Technical Support Departments, 269-276
Help key, 206
Help! (Teknosys), 38, 283-284
high-density floppy disks, 107, 110
Home key, 206
HP Deskwriter, 149
HyperCard
   files, saving, 127
   stacks, 39

I

icons
   lost, 145
   printing files from, 177-178
   Sad Mac, 103-118
ID numbers
   fonts, 180

SCSI device problems, 83
illegal characters, 216
ImageGrabber (Sebastian Software), 196
ImageWriters, 149
   using with IBM PCs, 166
imaging technologies, 10-11
importing data, 241-242
information services, 62
INITPicker (Microseeds Publishing), 26, 57, 284
INITs, 33, 50, 56-58
   HeapTool, 61
   turning off, 24-26
ink-jet printers, 10, 149-150
input devices, 11-12
   multiple, 222
   see also keyboards, mouse, trackballs
Installer program, 36-37
installing programs
   adding files to System Folder, 232-233
   manually, 231-232
   system software, 34-37
   see also reinstalling
internal modems, 252
InTouch (Advanced Software), 177
INtouch desk accessory, 265
isolation, program problems, 227

J-K

jamming
   floppy disks in drives, 117-118
   printers, 158

K (kilobytes), 7

key bounce, 216
Key Caps desk accessory, 213
Keyboard control panel, 215
keyboards, 5, 11-12
   no response to, 216-218
   types, 203-204
KeyFinder desk accessory (Norton Utilities for the Mac), 213-214
keys, 206-215

L

labels, printing, 165-166, 176-177
landscape mode, 159
laser printers, 10, 149-150
   dark/light printouts, 172-173
   double-sided printing, 167
   downloading fonts, 168-169
   Mac-compatible, 150
   no-print zone at edges of pages, 171-172
   PostScript files, creating, 170-171
   refilled cartridges, 173-174
   spacing between characters, 172
   white streaks, 173
line conditioning, 20
line-feed (LF), 262
lines, gray hairline on-screen, 194
linking files, 242
loading files, 95-96
local echo, 260-261
locked up Macintoshes, 217, 221-222
locking
   files, 145
   floppy disks, 119-120

About the Author

Dr. Steven Schwartz has been a computer industry writer for almost 15 years, writing extensively for publications such as *Macworld*. He is a major contributor to *The Macintosh Bible*, and was one of the founding editors of *Software Digest*, the Business Applications Editor for *MACazine*, a contributing editor for *Nibble* magazine, and the Director of Technical Services for Funk Software. Dr. Schwartz has written hundreds of articles and a dozen books — including *The 9-to-5 Mac* (Hayden Macintosh Library), a book/disk combination for increasing business productivity on the Mac.

Learn computers the easy way with PC Novice!

Learning to use computers is like anything new — getting started is the hard part. Now there's a computer magazine designed specifically to help you get started. It's called PC Novice — the only magazine that presents *Personal Computers In Plain English*. Every issue of PC Novice is packed with articles that explain the basic information you need to learn how to use your PC.

Need advice on how to computerize your business?

PC Today helps small businesses solve problems with computers. With pertinent article topics and an easy-to-read editorial style, PC Today keeps you entertained as well as informed. It's the best way you can find out about hardware and software that will give your growing business a competitive edge.